P9-BTM-756

*D*URING the past twenty years The Reader's Digest has published more than 8,000 articles.

When it was decided to commemorate our twentieth anniversary by reprinting in a book the best article from each year of the Reader's Digest, the task of selection loomed as a formidable one. But twelve men and women, all good judges of reading, agreed to help.

After the editors of The Reader's Digest had narrowed the choice to the most outstanding articles for each year, the final twenty were selected by Bruce Barton — John Erskine — John Kieran — Christopher Morley — William Lyon Phelps — Robert Sherwood — Dorothy Canfield — Helen Hayes — Paul de Kruif — Kathleen Norris — Mary Roberts Rinehart — and Lowell Thomas.

To the articles thus chosen was added the condensation of *"Madame Curie,"* considered by the editors of The Reader's Digest one of the finest book supplements they have ever published.

But no book would truly represent the Digest without selections from "Toward a More Picturesque Speech," "Patter," "Talk of the Town," and the one best from the popular series "The Most Unforgettable Character I Have Ever Met." Editors of these departments named their favorites for inclusion here.

The result is a veritable digest of The Reader's Digest—each article in its chronological order. Illustration and typography are new; but the text remains as it first appeared.

The editors believe that wherever you open this little book you will find eloquent confirmation of the statement on the cover of every issue:

"Articles of Lasting Interest"

THE
READER'S DIGEST
TWENTIETH ANNIVERSARY
ANTHOLOGY

THE READER'S DIGEST ASSOCIATION

PLEASANTVILLE, NEW YORK

～◈ CONTENTS ℰ～

The condensations reprinted in this book are used by permission of and special
arrangement with the publishers holding the respective copyrights

Copyright 1941 by The Reader's Digest Association, Incorporated

FIRST EDITION

*All rights reserved, including the right to reproduce this book
or parts thereof in any form*

808
R 286

Are You Alive?

Condensed from The Nation

Stuart Chase

There seems to be an ascending scale of values in life, and somewhere in this scale there is a line—probably a blurred one—below which one more or less "exists" and above which one more or less "lives."

I HAVE often been perplexed by people who talk about "life."

Americans, they tell me, do not know how to live, but the French—ah, the French—or the Hungarians, or the Poles, or the Patagonians. When I ask them what they mean by life they do not advance me an inch in my quest of the definition of life.

What does it mean to be alive, to live intensely? What do social prophets mean when they promise a new order of life? Obviously they cannot mean a new quality of life never before enjoyed by anyone, but rather an extension of vitality for the masses of mankind in those qualities of "life" which have hitherto been enjoyed only by a few individuals normally, or by large numbers of individuals rarely.

What is it which is enjoyed, and how is it to be shared more extensively? Can we hold life on a point for a moment while we examine it?

What, concretely, is this "awareness," this "well-being?" I want in a rather personal way to tell you the facts as I have found them. I want to tell you when I think I live in contradistinction to when I think I "exist." I want to make life very definite in terms of my own experience, for in matters of this nature about the only source of data one has is oneself. I do not know what life means to other people but I do know what it means to me, and I have worked out a method of measuring it.

I get out of bed in the morning, gulp coffee and headlines, demand to know where my raincoat is, start for the office—and so forth. These are the crude data. Take the days as they come, put a plus beside the

Selected from September 1922 issue of The Reader's Digest

5

17225

living hours and a minus before the dead ones; find out just what makes the live ones live and the dead ones die. Can we catch the verihood of life in such an analysis? The poet will say no, but I am an accountant and only write poetry out of hours.

My notes show a classification of eleven states of being in which I feel I am alive, and five states in which I feel I only exist. These are major states, needless to say. In addition, I find scores of sub-states which are too obscure for me to analyze. The eleven "plus" reactions are these:

I seem to live when I am creating something—writing this article, for instance; making a sketch, working on an economic theory, building a bookshelf, making a speech.

Art certainly vitalizes me. A good novel, some poems, some pictures, operas, many beautiful buildings and particularly bridges affect me as though I took the artist's blood into my own veins. There are times, however, when a curtain falls over my perceptions which no artist can penetrate.

The mountains and the sea and stars—all the old subjects of a thousand poets—renew life in me. As in the case of art, the process is not automatic—I hate the sea sometimes—but by and large, I feel the line of existence below me when I see these things.

Love is life, vital and intense. Very real to me also is the love one bears one's friends.

I live when I am stimulated by good conversation, good argument. There is a sort of vitality in just dealing in ideas that to me at least is very real.

I live when I am in the pressure of danger—rock-climbing, for example.

I feel very much alive in the presence of a genuine sorrow.

I live when I play—preferably out-of-doors at such things as diving, swimming, skating, skiing, dancing, sometimes driving a motor, sometimes walking.

One lives when one takes food after genuine hunger, or when burying one's lips in a cool mountain spring after a long climb.

One lives when one sleeps. A sound healthy sleep after a day spent out-of-doors gives one the feeling of a silent, whirring dynamo. In vivid dreams I am convinced one lives.

I live when I laugh—spontaneously and heartily.

In contradistinction to "living" I find five main states of "existence" as follows:

6

I exist when I am doing drudgery of any kind—adding up figures, washing dishes, answering most letters, attending to money matters, reading newspapers, shaving, dressing, riding on street cars or up and down in elevators, buying things.

I exist when attending the average social function—a tea, a dinner, listening to dull people talk, discussing the weather.

Eating, drinking, or sleeping when one is already replete, when one's senses are dulled, are states of existence, not life. For the most part I exist when I am ill.

Old scenes, old monotonous things—city walls, too familiar streets, houses, rooms, furniture, clothes—drive one to the existence level. Sheer ugliness, such as one sees in the stockyards or in a city slum, depress me intensely.

I retreat from life when I become angry. I exist through rows and misunderstandings and in the blind alleys of "getting even."

So, in a general way, I set life off from existence. It must be admitted of course that "living" is often a mental state quite independent of physical environment or occupation. One may feel—in springtime for instance—suddenly alive in old, monotonous surroundings. Then even dressing and dishwashing become eventful and one sings as one shaves. But these outbursts are on the whole abnormal. By and large there seems to be a definite cause for living and a definite cause for existing. So it is with me at any rate. I believe that I could deliberately "live" twice as much—in hours—as I do now, if only I would come out from under the chains of necessity—largely economic—which bind me.

I have indeed made some estimates of the actual time I have spent above and below the "existence" line. For instance, my notes show that in one week, of the 168 hours contained therein, I only "lived" about 40 of them, or 25 per cent of the total time. This allowed for some creative work, a Sunday's hike, some genuine hunger, some healthy sleep, a little stimulating reading, two acts of a play, part of a moving picture, and eight hours of interesting discussion with various friends.

It may be that the states of being which release life in me release it in most human beings. Generally speaking, one's salvation is bound closely with that of all mankind—the ratio of living, growing with that of the mass of one's fellow-men.

Personal Contact and Labor

Condensed from The Rotarian

Sherman Rogers

THE average theoretical labor expert makes the labor problem appear extremely complex. Such is not the case. The subject should be considered in the light of these four principles:

First, there are three sides to every question—your side, the other fellow's side, and the right side. I don't believe there was ever a question in either modern or ancient history where either side of a dispute was 100 per cent right. The labor problem is no exception. Whenever the employer and labor get together and compare notes, they will find the right side; and they will find that neither one of them was ever 100 per cent right.

Second, there was never a man big enough to hate and reason at the same time. There is a whole Bible in that statement.

Third, 95 per cent of men, regardless of whether they wear broadcloth or overalls, want to play the game square. Lack of contact means lack of understanding. Those engaged in practically all disputes are absolutely sincere, but lack of friendly association breeds suspicion, which in turn, breeds both fear and hate; and it is impossible under those circumstances to have a rule of reason.

Fourth, foremen have played the greatest part in American industry; and the trouble is that a great many of these under-executives, as Douglas Malloch says, "can only say 'well done' when ordering a T-bone steak."

I believe that the ambitions of more workmen have been crushed, the good will and spirit of more workmen buried by indifferent foremen than all other causes put together. I can say from real heart-deadening experience that in the old school of foremen there were mighty few who applied the human element, who ever dreamed of letting a workman know that his efforts were appreciated.

We condemn the agitator roundly, but he is only dangerous where the employer is at fault. He can only be the recognized friend of the worker where the management has refused to extend their friendship—either refused or didn't think they had time enough to be friendly. If

Selected from August 1923 issue of The Reader's Digest

the employers would spend as much time in cultivating the friendship, the respect, and the good will of labor as they do in fighting some labor organization, there wouldn't be a labor problem.

I am not dreaming in that statement either. Here is what I mean: I was working in the Seattle shipyards in 1917, when it was announced that Charles M. Schwab would speak on a certain date. For days the men on all sides denounced him as a labor hater, a bloated magnate. But, later, those 4,000 men in overalls completely forgot during the 30 minutes that Schwab talked that he was a rich man. He bared his heart. He tore aside the veil of misunderstanding. He destroyed at once the barrier of class distinction. And he received an ovation that few men have ever received. In that short 30 minutes he destroyed the hatreds that agitators had been building for 15 years.

The answer is simply *contact*. There isn't an employer living, if he really likes his men, that couldn't have delivered the same talk that Schwab did. It was a talk of monosyllables carried on in about the same tone and manner any business man would use in conferring with a friend.

I have noted all over America that wherever I found an employer who really likes his men, and means it, that employer has no trouble in conveying to them that he does like them. And those employers have mighty little difficulty in getting the whole-hearted respect and co-operation of practically every man on the payroll. Employers will never get respect by showing arrogance and indifference. The big thing is this: The employer generally has a strong personality. He has spent a lot of time selling his honesty, his fairness and his personality to the banker, the wholesaler, the retailer, and the public. How much time has he spent in trying to sell that same personality, honesty, and fairness to his workmen? The answer is the cause of most of the trouble in American industry.

I can name places by the score where, within a few years, a feeling of confidence and respect has taken the place of suspicion and hatred. These employers have simply taken off their coats, gotten right down in their plants, and have spent as much time cultivating the friendship and respect of their men as they have in cultivating that same feeling among their business and social acquaintances. And the employer who has done that has been amazed at the difficulties labor is confronted with. They have been amazed that there were so many grievances that they formerly knew nothing about—little grievances that later grew into big ones, and then grew into strikes, with more hatreds. These men

9

have given their men an equal chance with them in discussing the conditions under which the men work. These men have established industrial representation, in which labor elects representatives, by secret ballot, to represent them at a conference, where an equal number of employers' representatives are present, where they meet with equal power to discuss and settle all disputes that come up. This places labor in a position where an agitator simply cannot exist, because every statement by either side has recourse to a conference table, where things said must be proved. When an agitator knows that he is going to be made out a liar in a day or two if he does lie, he is going to be mighty careful with his tongue.

This system worked out well in manufacturing concerns of all kinds. They said it couldn't be used with the railroads. W. W. Atterbury had a different idea. He believed that if he could talk to his workmen and get their side of the case, and let them get his, where they could see the books any time they wanted to see them, that they would not only be loyal to the company, but the cooperation, respect, and the good will established would result in not only a higher state of efficiency, but uninterrupted railroad service to the entire country. What has been the result? When the big strike came along, wherever the company had gotten a chance to establish close contact, there were only a few strikers. In the localities where that contact had not been established, practically all men walked out. In Altoona 98 per cent stayed on the job; 70 per cent of the shopmen on the whole system stuck to their guns.

Solving a labor trouble is not a mysterious affair. It is simply a matter of using common sense. Confidence and co-operation must be inspired. It cannot be forced. Good will and respect must be inspired. It cannot be compelled. In other words, you can lead a good man through the fires of Hell, but you cannot drive him across the sidewalk.

You cannot prevent the birds of sorrow from flying over your head, but you can prevent them from building nests in your hair.
—Chinese proverb.

My Five Best Dinner Companions

Condensed from The American Magazine

Bruce Barton

HERE is an interesting thought: You and I will give a dinner to-night, and our guests shall be five men we choose, out of all who have ever lived.

Whom shall we invite? . . . Napoleon? He occupies the largest space in the biographical dictionaries, and if you insist on having him I will not be stubborn about it. But I warn you at the outset that he will spoil the dinner. He was a terrible failure, you know. His greed and selfishness destroyed his talents. He might talk interestingly at the table, but he can't talk sincerely; he will almost certainly be rude, and probably be a bore.

Shall we ask Caesar or Alexander? Or Croesus, who had so much money? or Charlemagne, who had so much power? All of them lived tumultuous lives and died by violence or in disappointment. We want no embittered old men at our supper; let's have men who succeeded, good companions, wealthy men. If you leave it to me to make up the list, I suggest these five:

 First in point of years, and perhaps of interest too, I should invite that homely old fellow, Socrates. He was so wealthy in common sense! Moving about from man to man, asking his sharp questions, puncturing the toy balloons of prejudice, he probably set men to thinking wherever he went. And his power still persists. "If you kill me," he said calmly and quite impersonally to his judges, "you will not easily find another like me, who, if I may use such a ludicrous figure of speech, am a sort of gadfly, given to the State by the gods; and the State is like a great and noble steed who is tardy in his motions, owing to his very size, and requires to be stirred into life." Socrates, surely, would put life into our party.

And, if for any reason he could not come, I would give a lot to see and hear that curious fellow countryman of his, Diogenes. He was the wealthiest of all who ever lived, for he wanted absolutely nothing. "Can I do anything for you?" asked Alexander the Great, standing in the doorway of the wooden tub in which the philosopher dwelt. "Yes," replied Diogenes briskly. "Get out of my sunlight."

Selected from August 1924 issue of The Reader's Digest

Dr. Samuel Johnson, because he was the world's richest talker. It was not as a talker that he hoped to be remembered. He wrote long, dull books, toiling terribly over them and expecting them to make him immortal. Nobody reads his books today, but his talk will live forever. Boswell has recorded it so perfectly that you almost see the ungainly form of the doctor and hear the rumble of his tones. He talked about everything, and always positively, with no doubt, no hesitation. When, very infrequently, the flow of words paused for a moment, Boswell was always ready with a suggestion to draw him out.

Boswell's father thought his son had wasted his life in tagging about after a penniless writer; and even Boswell himself complained a bit because the doctor kept such late hours and compelled him to absorb too much port wine. But a Mr. Dempster, about whom I know nothing except this one shrewd remark, reproved him sharply. "One had better be palsied at eighteen," he said, "than not to keep company with such a man."

Surely Sam Johnson must be in our company—a millionaire of good talk.

 For myself I should like to have Samuel Pepys come. No one will claim that he was ever great, but surely in one characteristic he was richer than any man who ever lived: He possessed a boundless and insatiable curiosity. Everything interested and thrilled him—everything. A wedding or a hanging; a new tune which he could try on his flute, a meeting of Parliament, a new suit of clothes, the rearranging of his books, the odor of a well-cooked meal—these were not merely the casual occurrences of ordinary life, they were adventures, all of them.

I pity anyone who can read his diary without discovering a new capacity for enjoyment in the things of everyday life. And yet he was more than a mere recorder of petty details. There are few finer passages in literature than the concluding sentences of his diary, whose writing he had to abandon because of the approach of blindness: "And so I betake myself to that course which is almost as much as to see myself go into the grave," he wrote, "for which, and all the discomforts that will accompany my being blind, the good God prepare me."

There was an element of the heroic in Samuel Pepys; but we are not inviting him as a hero. We want him because he would have seen so many curious and interesting things that we failed to see; and would tell about them so well.

I nominate Montaigne for our fourth guest, because he was so rich in the knowledge of himself. Emerson, on discovering Montaigne's essays, exclaimed, "It seemed to me as if I had myself written the book, in some former life, so sincerely it spoke to my thought and experience."

No franker writer ever lived than Montaigne; he was wholly free from self-deception. He observed that every man has deserved hanging five or six times, and confessed that he was no exception. "Five or six as ridiculous stories can be told of me as of any man living," he says. The sincerity of the man is inspiring; whatever happens he will not lie or equivocate; he will see and declare the truth.

Reading his words, which are so fresh and vivid after all the years, one finds new and thrilling areas within one's own consciousness. Knowing himself so well, declaring himself so completely, Montaigne discovers us to ourselves—a unique and splendid gift of service.

 Finally, I should like to have Abraham Lincoln with us, because he was so rich in patience and faith. Every year new books are published about him, until the number threatens to overtake the Napoleonic total. Each emphasizes a different aspect of his character. But through them all stands the wonder of his patience, which could wait without weariness or hopelessness, and of the faith that never lost its grip, or abandoned its power to smile.

You might choose an entirely different list of guests for your banquet of wealthy men; yet I imagine that your choice and mine would be alike in this—that those who were rich merely in money would not interest us. These five men owned the world; they were not owned by it. As Beecher owned every flower garden in Brooklyn, as Thoreau owned every orchard and bird and squirrel in Concord, as Pepys owned every exciting event in London, they possessed themselves of the experiences of all with whom they came into contact, of all good books, good talk, good thinking, and good friends. We are richer for being in their company. Richer in the only real wealth, which is Life.

One man with courage makes a majority.
—Andrew Jackson

13

YOU

Condensed from Scribner's Magazine

Edward W. Bok

Late editor and philanthropist; author of "The Americanization of Edward Bok," etc.

I F TIMID FOLK could only realize the potentiality that is implanted in each one of us—singly! These folk have aspirations, the urge to do. But, invariably, they are deprecatory, ever disparaging of self. They fall back upon the plaint: "I am just one man" or "one woman." "What can I do?"

What was Florence Nightingale but one woman? Yet her work led straight to the Red Cross! How far would be the humane processes of healing the wounded and sorrowful all over the world today had this English nurse sat down and bemoaned the fact that she was "just one woman"?

Where would the marvelous work done by radium be today if Madame Curie had folded her arms when her husband passed away and minimized herself by saying: "I am just one woman"?

Yes, but exceptional women, you say. Quite to the contrary. "I had faith: that was all," said Florence Nightingale. "I had confidence, little else," said Madame Curie, and to their work each applied her fullest aspiration and trust.

Was that mother "exceptional" whose six-year-old boy came home from school one day with a note from his teacher suggesting that he be taken from school as he was "too stupid to learn"? "My boy is not stupid," said the mother. "I will teach him myself." She did, and Thomas A. Edison was the result.

How often a woman says, "I am just a home body, busy with the daily task." . . . Abraham Lincoln's stepmother was "just a home body." But she taught and inspired the son of her husband—not even of her own blood—and held a torch before him which he carried to emancipate a people. "The greatest book I ever read, you ask me?"

Copyright 1925, Charles Scribner's Sons, 597 Fifth Ave., N. Y. C.
(Scribner's, October, '25)
Selected from October 1925 issue of The Reader's Digest

asked Lincoln in a letter. "My mother." So was Dwight L. Moody's wife "just a home body," but she taught her husband how to write, put the love of God and of his fellow men into his heart, and sent him forth as the greatest evangelical force of his century.

There was another wife whose husband had to leave home for an indefinite period, leaving his son in his wife's care. "I will take his father's place," she said. And she read to him of the achievements of the great men of his time and stirred his ambition. She implanted in him the highest ideals of Christianity. For years she did this; "just a home body." She produced Robert E. Lee.

We do not seem to get it into our heads that the great works of the world always begin with one person. Emerson put a sermon in a dozen words: "A great institution is but the lengthened shadow of a single man." A man disgusted with committees thus expressed a large truth: "The ideal committee consists of three, with two of the members ill." Every institution that has contributed to American progress has been built upon the initiative and enthusiasm of an individual.

We have become obsessed in this country with the idea that we cannot work alone: only in organization. Look at these organizations, and invariably the creative part, the driving power, is traced to the individual; oft-times, one: other times, two: rarely more. "Yes," it is agreed. "But these are greater than I am." "There are no great and small," says Emerson. "We fancy others greater than ourselves because they light the divine spark given them, and we do not. It is because we minimize ourselves that we do not accomplish. We do not realize the power of the positions in which we are placed."

Take this example: "I am just a teacher!" Fancy! In a belittling tone this is said of the greatest post of potential influence in life today next to a mother. So said once a teacher I know. Then the vision came to her. From that day her work in her class changed: her eye took on a new radiance to her children: her voice that of the supreme confidence which God gives to us all to bring into being. She had lighted the divine spark within her. Within 18 months she was principal of the entire school. Today into hundreds of hitherto perplexed eyes of the little foreigners in her school she has put a steady light: a true Americanization; and every June she is sending out into America a line of true little Americans who, within a few years, will register the teachings of this one woman at the ballot-boxes and in the homes of our land!

"O ye of little faith." That is where the trouble lies: either we have no faith at all, or we are "of little faith." What a sentence that is which

Jesus spake: "If ye have faith as a grain of mustard seed, nothing shall be impossible unto you."

I stand aghast at young men who busy themselves with introspective thoughts, full of argument of whether they can do this or that. Wasting their time. Instead of saying: "God put me here for some purpose. I am going to realize it." Once we are convinced of that single fact: that we are put here for a purpose: that the seed of divine energy has been given us and that it is for us to cultivate it to its fullest bloom, the way will be shown us. It is our part to make the effort and to put the fullest force and integrity into that effort. It is the young man of little faith who says, "I am nothing." It is the young man of true conception who says, "I am everything," and then goes to prove it.

Napoleon struck at the very foundations of all this when he said, "Circumstances? I *make* circumstances." That was not the word of an egotist. It was a fact. We *all* make circumstances.

The Art of Evasion

An actress was testifying in New York in a suit for damages, and the cross-examiner plotted to discredit all her testimony by proving that she consistently lied about her age. She was 52, but posed as being about 40. She didn't want to lie under oath.

"How old are you?" the cross-examiner asked.

"I don't know," she said promptly.

"What! You don't know?"

"No. I have never had a birth certificate. I have never looked up the record of my birth."

"But Miss —," the cross-examiner protested suavely, "surely your parents told you how old you are. When did they say you were born?"

"That," said the actress firmly, "is hearsay evidence and I am sure you would not ask that it be admitted."

"But . . . but . . ." the cross-examiner sputtered.

The actress turned to the judge. "Am I right or wrong, Your Honor?"

The judge grinned. "You are correct," he said.

—J. B. Griswold in *The American Magazine*

16

PICTURESQUE SPEECH

She had a tongue that would clip a hedge.

As hard to catch as a waiter's eye.

She was throwing herself away, perhaps, but she was taking careful aim.

The clock-hands were closing like scissor blades on midnight, snipping off another day.

Restless as a windshield wiper.

They clucked over their grains of gossip.

Her hat always looked as if it had made a forced landing upon her head.

She has a small mind but knows it thoroughly.

Irrevocable as a haircut.

A famous politician trying to save both his faces.

The secret was hushed about from place to place.

I won't be highbrow beaten.

She didn't want advice: she only used you as a waste basket for her worries.

The kind of man who remembers your age but forgets your birthday.

As unplanned as a hiccup.

Her look hung a price tag on every object in the room.

He dresses like an unmade bed.

As uncomfortable as an afterthought.

The slow punctuation of fireflies in the garden.

He's all sail and no anchor.

He looked like an accident going somewhere to happen.

He had a good memory and a tongue hung in the middle of it.

The bureaucratic squanderlust of our times.

Her hands dropped open, spilling dismay.

The full moon pushed the clouds aside as if they were double doors.

Genuine as a thumbprint.

Commander Byrd's Story

Condensed from The National Geographic Magazine

Rear Admiral Richard E. Byrd, U. S. Navy (Ret.)

O N May 9, 1926, Floyd Bennett and I looked down upon the North Pole from our monoplane, completely verifying Peary's observations, and demonstrating the feasibility of using airplanes in any part of the globe.

We observed thousands of square miles of the Polar Sea never before seen by man. We did not suffer any extraordinary hardships, nor can we claim any great personal achievement. We simply took advantage of the knowledge gained by three centuries of Arctic heroes and applied our Navy training to aviation, and so added a short paragraph to the story of man's conquest of the globe on which we live.

Peary's trip to the North Pole and back, begun in 1908, kept him out of touch with civilization for more than 400 days. Bennett and I left civilization early one morning, and returned on the afternoon of the same day.

In aerial exploration great attention to detail must be the order of the day. To the Expedition's flight engineer, Lt. G. O. Noville, goes the credit for so efficiently assembling the material that we lacked nothing after we reached Kings Bay.

Here we come to a very interesting thing about Arctic exploration by air. Hundreds of people, men and women, volunteered to go. We could have recruited an army of assistants. Civilization may have a softening influence, but the spirit of adventure is far from dormant in America today. We received many letters also from people who had no chance to go with us. One letter from a lady was typical. "Little do you realize," she wrote, "that thousands of people who have no chance of adventure live your adventure with you. Probably you have no idea what pleasure you give us."

Selected from October 1926 issue of The Reader's Digest

We selected for our flight a Fokker three-engine monoplane. One was available that had already flown 20,000 miles. It had 200-horsepower Wright air-cooled motors, any two of which would keep it up. It was 43 feet long in body, with a wing spread of 63 feet. Two 100-gallon gasoline tanks were set in the center of each wing; and two others, each holding 110 gallons, were carried in the fuselage. The additional gasoline we might need was carried in five-gallon cans. The plane's fuel consumption at cruising speed was 28 gallons per hour. It was capable of a speed as high as 117 miles an hour.

The members of the Expedition were of the volunteer type, and all young. . . . Their spirit is still a matter of wonder to me.

After arduous labor on the part of all hands, we left New York on April 5, 1926, with 50 men, six months' food, and 15,000 miles of coal on board. Captain M. J. Brennan and his three mates of our Merchant Marine did a fine job in taking that Shipping Board steamer *Chantier*, which had been laid up for years, to Spitsbergen and back, 10,000 miles, with a largely landlubber crew.

We arrived at Kings Bay on April 29, and found the Amundsen-Ellsworth-Nobile Expedition members well under way in their preparation to receive the great Italian dirigible *Norge*. This revelation of the energy of another air expedition had a tonic effect on the eager young American spirit of our crew.

Fate lost no time in placing serious obstacles in our path. The little harbor of Kings Bay was choked with ice, but skillful work by Captain Brennan brought the *Chantier* to anchor within 300 yards of the shore.

By laying heavy planks across the gunwales of our whaleboats we constructed a big raft. A change in tide began to close the lane we had opened among the heavy cakes of ice that blocked our course ashore. Yet by tireless work and unswerving determination, our men managed to prop that awkward body of the plane on its frail support, and ferried it in safety to the rugged beach. We were taking a tremendous chance in doing this, for had a wind sprung up, the pontoon would have been crushed or blown out to sea. As we had only one plane for our polar flight, a serious accident at this juncture would have been fatal to the whole project.

The plane's first attempt to take off for a trial flight ended in a snowdrift and it nearly upset—which would have upset the Expedition as well! A ski was broken to bits and the landing gear bent. Things then looked black, but the men refused to lose heart. A repair gang worked all night installing new skis, while the rest of the crew worked at the muscle-tearing task of leveling off the mile-long slide of snow down which we had to run for the take-off.

Final preparations were completed on May 8. W. C. Haines, a meteorologist loaned us by the U. S. Weather Bureau, told us that the weather was right. We warmed the motors; put the last bit of fuel and food aboard; examined our instruments with care. We were off, but alas, not up!

Our load proved too great, the snow too "humpy," the friction of the skis too strong a drag. The plane simply would not get into the air. We got off the end of the runway at a terrific speed, jolted roughly over several snow hummocks and landed in a snowdrift, coming within an ace of upsetting, which, of course, would have smashed the plane.

We took off hundreds of pounds of fuel to lighten the load, and concluded to work through the night lengthening and smoothing the runway. At the same time we would take out of the plane as much equipment as we could spare.

The weather was still perfect. We decided to try to get off as near midnight as possible, when the night cold would make the snow harder and therefore easier to take off from. Finally, at a half hour past midnight Greenwich time, all was in readiness to go. Bennett and I had almost no sleep for 36 hours, but that did not bother us.

There lay the sun in the general direction of our goal, beckoning us on. We decided to stake all on getting away—to give the *Josephine Ford* full power and full speed. A few handclasps from our comrades and—we raced down that runway. The rough snow ahead loomed near but we never reached it. We were off for our great adventure!

Beneath us were our shipmates—every one anxious to go along, but unselfishly wild with delight that we were at last off—running in our wake, waving their arms, and throwing their hats in the air.

We had a short-wave radio set operated by a hand dynamo, should we be forced down on the ice. A handmade sledge was also stowed in the fuselage, on which to carry our food and clothing should we be compelled to walk to Greenland. We had food for ten weeks. Our main staple, pemmican, consisting of chopped-up dried meat, fat, sugar and raisins, was supplemented by chocolate, pilot-bread, tea, malted milk, powdered chocolate, butter, sugar and cream cheese.

Other articles of equipment were a rubber boat for crossing open leads if forced down, reindeer-skin, polar-bear and seal fur clothes. boots and gloves, primus stove, rifle, pistol, shotgun and ammunition; tent, knives, ax, medical kit and smoke bombs.

Within an hour of taking the air we passed the rugged and glacier-laden land and crossed the edge of the polar ice pack. We looked ahead at the ice pack, gleaming in the rays of the midnight sun—a fascinating scene whose lure had drawn famous men into its clutches, never to return. It was with a feeling of exhilaration that we felt that for the very first time in history two mites of men could gaze upon her charms, and discover her secrets, out of reach of those sharp claws. Perhaps!

No one had ever navigated an aircraft with accuracy to a distant point in the Polar Sea, and we naturally wondered if we could do it. Though it was important to hit the Pole from the standpoint of achievement, it was more important to do so from that of our lives, so that we could get back to Spitsbergen, a target none too big. We could not fly back to land from an unknown position. We must put every possible second of time and our best concentration on the job of navigating, of flying a straight course.

. . . There was only one thing to do—to depend upon the sun. We had to use a sun-compass. This instrument was invented for our use by A. H. Bumstead, chief cartographer of the National Geographic Society. I do not hesitate to say that without it we could not have reached the Pole; it is even doubtful if we could have hit Spitsbergen on our return flight.

The principle of this instrument is a kind of reversal of that of the sundial. In the latter, the direction of north is known and the shadow of the sun gives the time of day. With the sun-compass, the time of day is known, and the shadow of the sun, when it bisects the hand of the 24-hour clock, indicates the direction of north (or any other desired).

Then there was the influence of the wind that had to be allowed for. If, for example, a 30-mile-an-hour wind is blowing at right angles to the course, the plane will be taken 30 miles an hour to one side of its course. This "drift" can be corrected by an instrument called the drift-indicator, which we had developed for the first naval transatlantic flight.

Exact Greenwich time was necessary, so we carried two chronometers that I had kept in my room for weeks. I knew their error to within a second. There seems to be a tendency for chronometers to slow up when exposed to the cold, so we had taken their cold-weather error.

As we sped along over the white field below I spent the busiest and most concentrated moments of my life. Bennett was steering, and every minute or two he would look to me, to be checked if necessary, on the course by the sun-compass. Once every three minutes I checked the wind drift and ground speed, so that in case of a change in wind I could detect it immediately and allow for it.

We had three sets of gloves which I constantly changed to fit the job in hand, and sometimes removed entirely for short periods to write or figure on the chart. I froze my face and one of my hands in taking sights with the instruments from the trapdoors. Ordinarily a frostbite need not be dangerous if detected in time and if the blood is rubbed back immediately into the affected parts.

When I felt certain we were on our course, I turned my attention to the great ice pack, which I had wondered about ever since I was a youngster. We were flying at about 2000 feet, and I could see at least 50 miles in every direction. There was no sign of land. If there had been any within 100 miles' radius, we could have seen its mountain peaks, so good was the visibility.

I noted that the temperature was 8 degrees above zero—only 24 below freezing. That was not so low as might be expected, but it was getting colder as we sped north.

The ice pack beneath was criss-crossed with pressure ridges, varying from a few feet to 50 or 60 feet in height, while the average thickness of the ice was about 40 feet. A flash of sympathy came over me for the brave men who had struggled northward over that cruel mass. . . . We passed leads of water recently opened by the movements of the ice, and so dangerous to the foot traveler, who never knows when the ice will open up beneath and swallow him in the black waters of the Polar Sea.

There were no bumps in the air. This was as we had anticipated, for the flatness of the ice and the Arctic temperature are not conducive to air currents. Had we struck an Arctic gale, I cannot say what the result would have been. Another advantage of spring and summer flying would be the 24-hour daylight.

It was time now to relieve Bennett at the wheel, not only that he might stretch his legs, but so that he could pour gasoline into the tanks from the five-gallon tanks stowed all over the cabin. Piloting was not difficult because of the smoothness of the air, and I was able to check myself on the course by holding the sun-compass in one hand and steering with the other. I had time now leisurely to examine the ice pack and eagerly sought signs of life, a polar bear, a seal, or birds flying, but could see none.

When Bennett had finished pouring gasoline, he took the wheel again, and I went back to the incessant navigating. So much did I sight down on the dazzling snow that I had a slight attack of snow blindness. But I need not have suffered, as I had brought along the proper kind of amber goggles.

We were opening unexplored regions at the rate of nearly 10,000 square miles an hour, and were experiencing the incomparable satisfaction of searching for new land. . . . The sun was still shining brightly. Surely fate was good to us, for without the sun our quest of the Pole would have been hopeless.

When our calculations showed us to be about an hour from the Pole, I noticed through the cabin window a bad leak in the oil tank of the starboard motor. Bennett confirmed my fears. He wrote. "That motor will stop." It was a big moment. Bennett suggested that we try a landing to fix the leak. But I had seen too many expeditions fail by landing, so we decided to keep on for the Pole with our two remaining motors, if necessary.

At 9:02 a.m., Greenwich civil time, our calculations showed us to be at the Pole! The dream of a lifetime had at last been realized. We headed to the right to take two confirming sights of the sun, then turned and took two more. After that we took some moving and still pictures, then went on for several miles, and made a larger circle to take in the Pole.

Time and direction became topsy-turvy at the Pole. When crossing it on the same straight line we were going north one instant and south the next! All directions became south from the Pole itself.

At 9:15 a.m. we headed for Spitsbergen. To our surprise, the motor with the oil leak never stopped because (as we afterward found out) the leak was caused by a rivet jarring out of its hole, and when the oil got down to the level of the hole it stopped leaking.

The reaction of having accomplished our mission, together with the narcotic effect of the motors, made us drowsy when we were steering. I dozed off once at the wheel and had to relieve Bennett several times because of his sleepiness. But that return trip was a momentous experience.

The wind began to freshen and change, and in an hour we were making over 100 miles an hour. The elements were surely smiling that day on us, two insignificant specks of mortality flying there over that great, vast, white area in a small plane with only one companion, deaf from the motors, just a dot in the center of 10,000 square miles of visible desolation.

We felt no larger than a pinpoint and as lonely as the tomb; as remote and detached as a star.

23

Here, in another world, far from the herds of people, the smallnesses of life fell from our shoulders. What wonder that we felt no great emotion of achievement or fear of death that lay stretched beneath us, but instead, impersonal, disembodied. On, on we went. It seemed forever onward. I realized fully then that time is only a relative thing. An instant can be an age, an age an instant.

We were aiming for Grey Point, Spitsbergen, and finally, when we saw it dead ahead, we knew that we had been able to keep on our course!

It was a wonderful relief not to have to navigate any more. We came into Kings Bay flying at about 4000 feet. That tiny village was a welcome sight, but not so much so as the good old *Chantier*. I could see the steam from her welcoming and joyous whistle.

In a few moments we were in the arms of our comrades, who carried us with wild joy down the snow runway they had worked so hard to make.

The Postman's Ring

The postman seemed to our romantic childhood the most entirely enviable and likable creature in trousers. He could ring any bell he liked without a thought of running away. Nobody objected. On the contrary, you looked out for him, hoping that he would ring at your door. The longer he paused there, the better you liked him. It meant that he had such a lot of letters for you that it took him a long time to find them all. And of course the more letters there were the more joy there must be.

That is the miracle with the postman. He brings bad news and good news and indifferent news, but we can only remember him by the good news. Like the sundial he records only the sunny hours. He is the hope that springs eternal in the human breast. He comes up the path, probably with a handful of bills and other things that you would be pleased to do without. But nothing affects your faith in him. If he pass by your gate you are not grateful that he has not brought you ill news. You suspect that something pleasant has unaccountably gone askew. When we have ceased to want to hear the postman's ring we may conclude that we have seen the best of the day, and that the demon of disillusion has us in thrall. It is to have given up hope the legendary ship of our childhood will ever come home.   —A. G. Gardiner in *Many Furrows*

Franklin in Paris

Condensed from McNaught's Monthly

Phillips Russell

WHEN at the age of 70 Benjamin Franklin arrived in Paris, where he was to remain for nearly nine years as the American representative, he soon found time to write to Elizabeth Partridge of Boston as follows:

"Somebody it seems gave it out that I loved Ladies, and then everybody presented me their Ladies (or the ladies presented themselves) to be embraced, that is to have their necks kissed. For as to kissing of lips or cheeks it is not the mode here, the first is reckoned rude, and the other may rub off the Paint. The French Ladies have however 1000 other ways of rendering themselves agreeable; by their various Attentions and Civilities, and their sensible conversation."

There is perceptible in this letter a foretaste of the exhilaration which Franklin was to feel on being set down in a social milieu exactly suited to his tastes. Here he found women not only inextinguishably feminine, but cultured enough to appreciate his oracular sayings, leisured enough to sit for hours at his feet—and sometimes on his knees; and practiced in all those gracious arts which few of his hard-worked countrymen had had either the instinct or the cash to cultivate.

The hour of the French Revolution, in which so many of his friends were to perish, was approaching. Paris was deliriously squandering the wealth skimmed from the toil of millions of workmen and peasants. The upper-class men of France were busy with a thousand money-making, power-winning intrigues, leaving their women bored, and in a mood to welcome this novelty from the New World.

Franklin made the most of the opportunity which his immense prestige had won for him. He ejected from his memory the Poor Richardisms of his young manhood; shed the horny integument of a colonial shopkeeper and politician; and stood forth, with the adaptiveness which had been one of his most distinguishing traits, as a

Selected from March 1927 issue of The Reader's Digest

courtier, diplomat, and squire of dames—suave, mirthful, expansive, roguish to a degree. Crowds gathered at a respectful distance when he appeared in the streets. Medallions bearing his likeness were purchased and treasured. Proud houses opened eager doors at his approach. Learned men became credulous in his presence, and lovely women flouted distinguished followers to call him *"très cher papa."*

Years previously he had committed certain "errata" for which the moralists of Puritan America eyed him askance. For the purpose, no doubt, of strengthening his personal structure at its weaker points, he had drawn up for himself a creed composed of the following points: temperance, silence, order, resolution, frugality, industry, sincerity, justice, moderation, cleanliness, tranquility, chastity and humanity. There is no evidence that while in Paris he sinned against cleanliness, but some of the others suffered at least a temporary eclipse.

His cellar at Passy contained more than 1000 bottles of well-chosen vintages. He taught his French friends a boisterous drinking song which he had laid aside for 40 years. He dined out six nights a week, and to his lady friends he addressed letters which have scandalized biographers.

Franklin, however, did not lose his head. Amid the towering coiffures, the whitened wigs, the glittering sword blades and the velvet cloaks of Paris, a pawky something—perhaps an old showman's instinct—caused him to appear in public with straight, unpowdered hair, russet dress, and a cap of backwoods fur in the style made famous by Davy Crockett.

Nor did he neglect his real job, which consisted in maintaining the prestige and credit of the far-off new republic. He repeatedly raised indispensable loans, circulated incessant propaganda, outfitted cruisers, settled disputes, and kept the British ambassador sulking in obscurity.

Meantime he explored the 1000 manners by which, as he said, the ladies of France knew how to render themselves agreeable. He held his own against the most gifted beaux of *la belle France*. He was in turn father, uncle, confessor, and hovering lover. He charmed the young with his sportive lightness; he made the old laugh with his unblushing effrontery. Mme. Helvetius, in whose salon he was a favorite, was provoked to write him, apropos the possibility of their both rejoining their deceased mates in heaven: "but I believe that you, who have been a *coquin,* will be restored to more than one."

Among other feminine admirers of Franklin were the Duchesse d'Enville, the Comtesse d'Houdetot, Mme. de Forbach, Mme. Lavoisier, Mlle. Flainu, and Mme. Brillon. The last-named was a woman of undoubted brilliance and force of character. Franklin, who dined at her home twice a week, paid rather ardent court to her, but in her he more than met a match. She kept him at arm's length with the greatest skill and humor, and even declined to consider a marriage between her daughter and Franklin's son, an alliance upon which he was decidedly bent. Nevertheless, she seems to have had a very genuine affection for him, for in after years the American Philosophical Society came into possession of 119 letters written by her to the festive doctor. She once wrote, "I find in your letter evidence of your friendship and a tinge of that gaiety and gallantry which make all women love you. Your proposal to carry me on your wings, if you were the Angel Gabriel, made me laugh, but I would not accept it . . . ."

We must not take these passages too seriously. In these merry tilts with French dames he was merely responding to the demands of the age, and giving his nimble pen good practice.

Eight and a half years after Franklin had landed in France, Cornwallis suddenly surrendered at Yorktown, and *Très Cher Papa's* mission was at an end. Painfully—for his most frugal admonitions to his countrymen had not averted gout in himself—he set off for Havre in a litter lent by the Queen of France—loved and pampered to the last by ladies.

Franklin wrote his many maxims in an endeavor to incite himself, if possible, to obey them. He was naturally slothful, careless, improvident, bibulous and amative. He successfully concealed these weaknesses by preaching against them until he was sufficiently powerful, through the acquisition of property and position, to worry about them no longer. Like the good American that he was, he loved to publish precepts for the other fellow to obey.

His frequent falls through his own shop window had the effect of rendering him tolerant, sagacious, and amiable. He acquired a mellowness and ripeness of observation which, added to his natural shrewdness, made him highly companionable. He increased in stature as the years went by. He despised superstition, war and cant. He was avid in pursuit of truth, knowledge and recipes for cheese-making. He helped to drive squalor out of municipalities and a decent comfort into the average home. By his example rather than by his hard and dismal precepts, he showed men that achievement comes less by hard work than by keeping one's eyes open. He everywhere introduced good books, good printing and good conversation. One of the finest traits of his matured character was his generous appreciation of excellent women. He was a tremendous lover of the world and its people. He was our first civilized public man.

Extern

Condensed from The Century Magazine

Charles Anthony Robinson

O N the register of the Lying-In Hospital I was an extern in obstetrics, but to my colleagues on the District and my chief, I was just another baby-snatcher—and a pretty verdant one at that. In the traditional manner of Harvard medical students I, with three other stripling 'prentices, was fulfilling my obstetrical requirements by delivering babies in the slums of Boston. The District ran to the water-front on the south; on the west it was fringed by railroad yards; and far to the east it ended smack up against the stench and desolation of the city abattoir. This was our terrain; in this area of reeking tenements, flooded cellars, dives, alleys, piers and passageways, we delivered in one summer exactly 101 babies, and lost only one. And there was greater mourning among the baby-snatchers for the one that was lost, than rejoicing over the 100 that were justly delivered.

Fancy babies of the silver-spoon species have often cost their parents upwards of a thousand dollars. But in the District all babies are admitted gratis, else they would never be admitted at all. As student obstetricians we received no fees, and were allowed to accept no gratuities. We paid for our own food and transportation. We lost our own sleep and wore out our own shoe-leather ushering black, yellow and white babies into the world. After a month in the District we were bundles of raw nerves. But for every penny we spent and for every pound we lost, we gained an unpurchasable experience of medicine and a first-hand feeling for humanity.

The young extern going on his first assignment carries a bag of instruments, an instruction book, a flash-light and a pious realization of his own ignorance. True, he has examined all the diagrams, and has gone through all the maneuvers with a dummy torso and a baby doll. He is armed with the assurance that 88 percent of all children are born normally, and would be delivered perfectly whether he were in attendance or not. He knows further that in the case of an abnormal

Selected from April 1928 issue of The Reader's Digest

birth, a telephone call will bring immediate assistance from his chief. He knows all this, but the knowledge does not prevent him from being as nervous as a rooky under his first barrage.

My first evening on duty began slowly. I reported to Dr. Challoner, the House Officer. This "H. O." was himself a young doctor; sentimentality was not his failing.

"Remember," said he, "you're on an important service; it calls for patience, nerve, and at the proper time, *action*. We realize that you are not an expert. But you've got the rudiments of a brain, and we ask you to use it. Now these women who are to be your patients are for the most part foreigners, usually ignorant and almost always dirty. But I want you to give them every care and attention you'd give a Social Register matron. And mind you, no superior airs. Don't make the mistake of thinking that you're doing these women a favor. Ignorant as they are, they are contributing greatly to your education as a doctor, and for every hour you spend with them you're being rewarded ten times over. Another thing; they think you are a full-fledged doctor, and never permit them for a moment to think otherwise. Actually you *are* a doctor, with a permit from the State. When you step over the threshold of a house, take command. Get out in front and stay there, or else you'll find the neighborhood midwife putting it all over you, or perhaps a stevedore husband will decorate the ceiling with your viscera Lastly, preserve asepsis! Boil everything, scrub up six times over, otherwise your patient will get Rocky Mountain spotted fever—or something worse. That's all. Now stand by for a call."

I stood by, or rather fidgeted about until nine o'clock taking last glances at my charts, asking my two confrères as many questions as I dared. They were veterans of two weeks' service, with records of nine and ten babies respectively; for an hour they alternated in giving me hypodermic jabs of advice. Seeing me nervous, one of them finally came in with, "There's really nothing to it, big boy. After the first seven hours it's a cinch. Of course, if pre-eclamptic toxemia sets in, and the blood pressure hits 250—or in case it's triplets—why God help you. But otherwise you won't have much trouble. You'd better hit the mattress for a blink of sleep."

Nevertheless, when the telephone rang I was at the receiver before the bell stopped vibrating. A heavy frightened foreign voice clotted the wire with jumbled noises. Finally I gathered that some one's Minnie was having a baby, and that I was wanted quick.

"Name and address?"

"Jake Sidoloufkos, 14 Beeler Street. Come quick."

"I'll be right over. Get some water boiling."

I read Minnie's prenatal history in the clinical register: a Lithuanian, had married a Greek, was 24 years old, the mother of four children, all previous births normal, no toxic history—apparently everything was O. K. I ran out into the street. It was 10 o'clock. I couldn't have stood the suspense of a trolley, so I scared up a taxi, and after 15 minutes of jouncing and getting lost in alleys, the driver brought me to a darkened barracks on a miserable lane.

I ran up one, two, three flights of stairs, knocking and shouting, "Sidoloufkos; hey Jake Sidoloufkos." But my shouts echoed through an abandoned house. Leaping again down the rickety stairs, I noticed a light filtering through a crack in the basement floor. My pocket light (I learned then its importance in modern medicine!) showed me an entrance, and I entered the most desolate human habitation I had ever seen. I was to see many more such rooms, but the awful squalor of that dwelling place struck me with raw force. Pushing myself through a clump of neighbors who had gathered for the fracas, I found my patient sharing a sheetless bed with three sleeping children. She was in a deep coma, and even in my excitement I knew that her pulse was pounding dangerously. My blood-pressure apparatus registered 220. A hospital case, and no mistake. My instructions were to call the H. O. immediately. I looked around that room for one intelligent face—and saw not one. "Does anyone here speak English?" No answer. I bolted for the street, and ran till I saw the red lamp of a police station, and in another 30 seconds I had shot an emergency call to the H. O.

He arrived in a sweat with the "big bag" ten minutes later. One glance at Minnie's face confirmed my diagnosis. "Get an ambulance. If she lives till we get her to the hospital, she's lucky."

At this juncture Mr. Jake Sidoloufkos seemed to apprehend that all was not well with his Minnie. It was necessary to get his consent before we could move his wife to the hospital. While I ran for the ambulance, Challoner debated with him. Jake didn't want his wife to go to the hospital. She had already given birth to four children without the aid of an ambulance, and he was convinced that if she put her mind to it, she could do it again. Finally, after I had returned and cleared the room, Challoner won Jake's reluctant consent. We could have reached the same conclusion more directly with a black-jack.

While we were haranguing Jake, the ambulance clanged up; we put Minnie in on a stretcher, and were off, I perched beside the driver.

After escaping from the alleys we hit real pavement and the speedometer climbed to 50. "Yank that gong," said the driver. I yanked continuously—and felt like a conquering hero. Theater crowds parted like a Red Sea trough before our clanging chariot. Street crossings were blurs of red and green lights. Clang, clang, gangway for Life, Death and the Baby-snatchers—now I know why ambulance drivers stay ambulance drivers. In a few minutes Minnie was in the surgical amphitheater. Dennis, the good Dennis, the Caesarean marvel, was laying off his antiseptic field on Minnie's abdomen—Challoner was dousing the ether pads—and half an hour later I was trying to explain to Jake Sidoloufkos that his wife had just given birth to twins by a Caesarean section.

For the next month I lived, breathed and *was* the District. It belonged to me, and I belonged to it. The dreary alleys that were the lairs of tom-cats and the refuge of garbage barrels, became the avenues of my profession. I was no longer a neophyte. I was eye to eye with life, a full-fledged, double-barreled baby-snatcher with 12 babies—three of them pickaninnies—to my credit. I no longer trembled at the thought of twins. No longer did I spray ether on my coat to impart a professional aroma. The District claimed me for 18 or even 20 hours a day. I was not only the Doctor, but the spiritual confidant and adviser, the job-finder, the friend and often the financier of some poverty-stricken home. No one in the District has any money, or ever will have. Few of the men have jobs; many of them are, were, or will be, in jail. Life in the District has no upward curve; no joyous sweep into the light of health and prosperity. It drops forever downward, or at best moves miserably along on a level below the meanest conceivable standard of existence.

A baby-snatcher soon learns that he must work with what comes to hand. In his battle against infection, boiling water is his chief aid—sometimes boiled in a borrowed kettle, on a neighbor's stove, over fuel that the extern has purchased. Towels, bed linen, layettes are fables all. Many an infant has to be wrapped in newspapers, because there is not a shred of cloth in the house. Rats eat the doctor's soap; roaches swarm—and yet in the midst of these social swamps, mother love and paternal anxiety struggle to lift the infant, for an hour at least, out of the stagnant scum and the miasmic steam. But I do not remember a single instance where my instructions to the mother or my job-hunting zeal for the father produced a change for the better. The specific gravity of the District is heavy as death itself, and no third-year medical student can hope to free a single victim from its grasp.

In addition to the actual delivering of babies, the baby-snatcher must keep in touch with his "cases" to see that no complications set in. For the first three days he must make three calls a day; for the next week he must make at least one daily call. A normal case was usually discharged after 10 days. We used to try to make the mothers stay in bed during this period, but no amount of persuasion could keep them off the floor.

One morning at daybreak, when on my way back to the Clinic, I saw a familiar figure walking through the morning mist. She was carrying a bundle in her arms and crooning a strange Celtic lullaby. Oblivious to everything but the living warmth at her breast, she passed me; turning, I called her by name.

"Mrs. Delehanty," I said, "don't you remember me?"

"Why sure," said she, "it's the Doctor. How could I forget the doctor that brought me my little Willy. Here now, look at the darlin'." And she pulled the shawl away from Willy's pinched blue face. He looked like a hungry infant not yet three weeks old—which was just what he was.

I couldn't account for her five o'clock rambling. "Where've you been?" I asked her.

"Oh, working. I got a fine job for myself over in the city there. I scrub bank floors at night, so I can be with my kids in the daytime. But I have to feed Willy, so I take him with me, and lay him right on the president's own chair. He likes it—Willy does, I mean."

In the presence of this scrubwoman I felt suddenly and completely unimportant. "Well, take care of yourself, Mrs. Delehanty!" I said, realizing the inanity of my remarks. Apparently Mrs. Delehanty did not. She went on her way crooning softly, stopping every twenty paces to peep under her shawl and glory in the possession of Willy.

In Memoriam

Calvin Coolidge's inscription in a friend's book, after the death of Calvin Coolidge, Jr.: "To my friend, in recollection of his son and my son, who, by the grace of God, have the privilege of being boys throughout Eternity."

On the bank of the James River, a husband erected a tombstone in memory of his wife, one of those 100 maidens who had come to Virginia in 1619 to marry the lonely settlers. The stone bore this legend:

"She touched the soil of Virginia with her little foot and the wilderness became a home."

—Eudora Ramsay Richardson, *The Influence of Men* (Bobbs-Merrill)

I Am Fifty
—and It Doesn't Hurt!

Condensed from The American Magazine

Dorothy Canfield

Do you remember the little girl who asked if it didn't feel queer for a few days after you grew up? I think of her when people ask me how I feel about being middle-aged. The answer is, "You don't feel anything sensational. You just go on living."

Of course I realize that I am no exception to the laws which make all women around 50 very different from what they were at 20. To take, first, the most obvious change, and one that has always provided a theme for melancholy poems—the inexorable passing of the smooth-skinned, bright-haired radiance of youth. Why have I been so little troubled by this change?

The 1914-18 war taught me a lesson on that point. I spent much time in France, in contact with the direst needs. We, who were doing what we could to help, desperately needed reinforcements. To be of any use, our reinforcements must be capable of endurance, perseverance, self-forgetfulness. We came to distrust bright eyes and gleaming young hair. In our minds these pretty signs of physical youth became associated with childishness, fickleness, lack of conscience. We could not always provide the "something exciting" without which they would not stick at a long, tiresome job till it was done. Would not? Apparently they could not. For dependability is a quality almost impossible to youth, but natural to the middle-aged tastes.

Remembering the heartfelt liking we had in our war work for the plain, middle-aged faces of the women who could be counted on to stick it out, no matter what came, I do not now feel desolately that the world has no more welcome for me.

A young poet would, of course, be horrified at my resigned satisfaction. But bring to mind the fact that 99.5 percent of good lyric poetry always has been written by young people who are brilliantly improvising on a subject they know nothing about.

Selected from May 1929 issue of The Reader's Digest

Being middle-aged is a nice change from being young. Honestly, I mean it. One of the traits of human nature about which there is unanimity of opinion is its love for change. When I was a young lady—that is what we were 30 years ago—I was anything but superior to the pleasures of young ladyhood. I "adored" opening the long pasteboard box which meant a bouquet from an admirer. I loved maple-nut sundaes to distraction, and there never was a girl, I am sure, who more heartily delighted in West Point hops. But suppose that by some miracle I should now look young again, and should be invited to dance once a week for the rest of this session at West Point, as I used to do. I'd rush into it as enthusiastically as I should carry out a sentence to play tag for an hour a day.

I still quite naturally enjoy playing tennis, riding horseback, skating, and mountain climbing. It is true I don't engage in these sports as ferociously as I did at 20, and for a good reason. I don't need to, or care to. At 20 I was like nearly everybody else of that age, frightfully uncertain—half of the time at least—of deserving to be in the world at all, and as a result was frightfully anxious to prove my worth to myself in the only way youth knows—by beating somebody else at something.

Here is one of the pleasures of middle age of which nobody breathes a word to you beforehand: the deliciousness of outgrowing that neuralgia of youthful pain at being surpassed in anything. This change is not due to greater magnanimity—rather to the fact that moderately successful, healthy-minded older people have found an excuse for existence in some job that the world seems to want done, which, after a fashion, they seem competent to do.

My gentle old uncle, when the cat had settled down to sleep in his favorite soft chair, used always to leave her there and sit upon a hard chair till she woke up and went away. When we remonstrated with him, he answered, "A cat has so few pleasures compared with those open to me." I have something of the same feeling about the boy who beats me in a race on the ice. He does *so* enjoy beating somebody. And there is so much else that I can enjoy of which he doesn't dream. For one thing, I can consciously, disinterestedly, relish the physical delights of the exercise, the miraculous knife-edge poise, the gliding speed, the tingling air, the beauties of the frosty trees. I enjoy these things far more than he does, or than I did at his age, freed as I am now from his single reason for being on the ice: either beating, or learning to beat, somebody else.

Understand me, I do not make the claim that I enjoy my corner of the pond *more* than that magnificent, long-legged kid out there, racing from one end of the hockey field to the other in eagle-like swoops. He is enjoying a wild, physical intoxication which gets considerably dimmed by the years. But as far as that goes, his physical intoxication is not so wild as that of a group of quite little children who, with faces of pure joy, are merely scuffling along on a slide at one end of the pond. The point is that we are all, in different ways suitable to our ages, having a glorious time. The young couple who swing dreamily around and around, hands clasped, are not the only ones to enjoy the ice.

I use skating, of course, as a convenient symbol for the way life is taken at different ages. Now, you will note that of all those age-groups on the ice, I, being the oldest, am the only one who has any notion that *everybody* is having a good time. Although the 14-year-old kid may be amused by "the kids without even any skates," he is not sorry for them, because he remembers that ages ago he used to enjoy sliding. But it is real pity he feels for the poor fish who's got tied up with a girl and has to steer her around. And probably his pity is even greater for the gray-haired woman who seems to think that cutting circles is skating. The young couple know, of course, that the hockey-playing boys who have not yet found their mates are having some sort of childish good time, but they are convinced that it must be awful to be so old as to have gray hair, with your first love far behind you.

The trouble, you see, is that they don't trust the future. Young people seldom do. They are afraid to. They are so impressed with the present that what they can't get now, this instant, seems lost forever.

Is it true, as people say, that youth is naturally happier than age because the one lives on hopes, the other on memories, and that while you can change hopes to suit yourself, memories persist in staying more or less the way they actually happened? Stuff and nonsense! Hope's always left, no matter what afflictions have come out of Pandora's box. It's not a question of an age limit. From cradle to grave the favorite slogan of every mother's son and daughter is: "I've learned my mistakes. Hereafter everything I tackle is going to go over big."

The fear of approaching old age? Having arrived at an age which seemed to me at 20 as forlorn as 80 does to me now, and perceiving that a change of tastes and desire has gone along with a change in age, I cannot help guessing that if I continue to yield myself naturally to the rhythm of the years, I shall find the inner time-table making as close and accurate connection for me then as now.

THE TALK OF THE TOWN

Excerpts from The New Yorker

Souvenir of Mexico

Two pretty, earnest young school teachers went to Mexico last summer; they avoided all the tourist places, desiring only the real flavor of Mexico. They got it, too. Arriving in a highly flavored little inland city, they set out to explore. Coming to a street mellifluously named the Avenue of the Beautiful Springs and the Waterfall and the Bridge That Is Music in Stone, they turned into it, only to be pounced upon by a policeman and haled off to the police station. There the captain explained that their offense was trespassing on the red-light district. There was a fine of 300 pesos for any girl caught without a license on the Avenue of the Beautiful Springs and the Waterfall and the Bridge That Is Music in Stone.

The girls protested that they were simply sightseeing and had no idea of muscling in, but the captain said the fine remained. Then he had an inspiration. "The fine is 300 pesos, but the license costs only 25. Why don't you apply for licenses?" he asked. The girls thought this a fine idea. For the Mexican equivalent of $5 each, they received handsomely engraved documents giving them access to the Avenue of the Beautiful Springs, etc.

Taxidermist

Three bright little boys entered the Metropolitan Museum one day, and made for the Egyptian exhibits, where they told an attendant they had come to see "the dead men." He showed them where the mummies were, and they stood in front of the cases for about 15 minutes, just looking. As they were going out, one of the innocents approached the attendant and asked, "You kill them and stuff them yourself?"

Props

This comes to us from a fine woman in Chicago. It seems that the junior boys of *the* settlement house in Chicago—you know the one—were rehearsing "Treasure Island" and found themselves without enough guns for the defense-of-the-stockade scene. Next night one of the youths showed up with a bulky newspaper package. It contained seven .32-calibre automatics. "We c'n use 'em for the rehearsals," he said, "but not for the show. The men gotta have 'em back Saturday night."

Pin Money

The fatherly president of a big publishing house called one of his young men on the carpet recently. "You're dressing pretty expensively," he said, "and last night I saw you having supper at the Plaza. Don't you think that's flying too high for $27.50 a week?"

"Oh, not at all," the young man said. "You see, I really make between $50 and $60 a week by raffling off my check to people in the office."

Dr. Post

It is customary in all big hospitals to notify the staff when an interesting post-mortem is to take place. It would be too blatant to have somebody shout, "Postmortem! Post-mortem!" through the public address system, and the usual solution is to pass the word along from doctor to doctor.

At one hospital, however, they have found a way to announce it over the loudspeakers. "Calling Dr. Post," the loudspeaker says, whenever something interesting is afoot in the autopsy room. "Calling Dr. Mortimer Post."

Service

Miss Anne Morgan's secretary was on her way home from a vacation and between trains in Chicago dashed off a postcard to her sister. "I hope I make this train," she concluded hurriedly, and handed the card to a Red Cap, asking him to mail it. When her sister got the card it bore a neat penciled postscript: "She made it. Respectfully yours, Red Cap."

Distinction

In a lower Fifth Avenue department store, on a hot day, a woman shopper was seen holding her lapdog up for a drink at one of the fountains stationed here and there through the aisles. A manager, advised of this, hurried to the scene. "My dear Madam," he said, "this fountain is for the use of customers." The lady looked contrite. "Oh, I *am* sorry," she replied in undoubted sincerity. "I thought it was for employes."

The Death Detail

Condensed from The World Tomorrow

William Pickens

Field Secretary of National Association for Advancement of Colored People

IT IS seldom that we get a clear look behind the curtains of military secrecy and see what happened "in time of war." But by a mere accident we are privileged to present, in the words of an eye-witness, the trial and the simultaneous execution of 13 Negro soldiers of the 24th Infantry, at Fort Sam Houston, Texas, December, 1917.

We give this narrative in the words of a northern white boy, a soldier of Company C, 19th Infantry, which guarded the Negro prisoners during the trial and execution. He gives us a clear picture: first, of the patience, regularity, deliberation, fairness and exceeding informality of such a military court; second, of the good sportsmanship and utter humanness of the white guards of the 19th Infantry; and third, of the qualities of the Negro soldier.

It is a story of a cold-blooded military trial and of the dramatic execution, simultaneously by hanging, of 13 men, an account that is all the more valuable because it was not written for publication. It is a simple newsy letter sent by an American soldier to his family in the North. A copy of his letter, with its informal but most effective narrative of actions and emotions, drifted around in the hands of one of his white comrades for 12 years, finally arriving in Havana, Cuba, where it stirred the imagination of a friend of mine, who sent it back to the United States. Here is the letter:

"Fort Sam Houston
"December 20, 1917

"... The court consisted of three brigadier generals and nine colonels. The judge advocate occupies the same position as our civil prosecuting

Copyright 1930, The World Tomorrow, Inc.
Selected from June 1930 issue of The Reader's Digest

attorney. The counsel for the defense is a commissioned officer selected by the accused. Major Grier defended the Negroes in a very creditable manner.

"From what I have been told, Major Grier taught military law at West Point for quite a while. I mention this merely to emphasize the fact that the government spared nothing in order that the colored men might get a fair trial. The first thing that occurs to a spectator at a military court is its fairness. The 13 members of the court are men who have received their education in different sections of the country; such men are free from this Southern prejudice.

"Now what part of this court is unlike our jury? We might say that each member of the court is a prosecuting attorney and a counsel for the defense, meaning that a member of the court can cross-question a witness or any of the accused in the same manner as the prosecution or defense. I need not explain why this is a benefit to a man who is innocent and a black eye to one who is guilty. All the flowery, spellbinding oratory in the world is just a waste of breath.

"Just a brief word as to my understanding of the riot. A Houston civil policeman for some reason or other attempted to arrest a colored woman. A Negro soldier who was passing by, protested to the policeman not for arresting her but for using what he thought was unnecessary violence, whereupon the officer at once arrested him. A colored military police appeared (Corp. Baltimore) and demanded the release of the soldier. The policeman struck the Military Police, saying, 'Do you want some of this too?' A false report soon reached the Negro camp that Corporal Baltimore had been killed by a Houston policeman. As the latter had attacked other soldiers unfairly at different times, and protests had fallen on deaf ears, the men decided to go to town and take the law into their own hands. They mutinied, made a rush on the ammunition tent, and started off to finish the job they had planned.

"The trial appeared to be one-sided. The defense had hardly an inch to stand on. Strangely enough, every man pleaded not guilty. The trial lasted exactly one month.

"I might mention the spirit of these men while confined and under the strain. What kept them in good cheer from beginning to end was their ability to sing. I honestly believe there was not a poor singer among the entire 64. Everyone in the guardhouse was anxious to hear their songs, and all the guards who were not on duty jammed themselves against the steel bar door which led into the prisoners' room.

"The spiritual welfare of the men was cared for by the Negro

Y. M. C. A., and by an old white haired French priest; and every colored church in the vicinity sent its members to the guardhouse to sing and pray. They formed themselves outside the building, some of them with tambourines, others playing violins. What a treat this was to the confined prisoners!

"I'm sending you a photograph of 'Big Frank Johnson.' This man was six feet six inches in height, weight about 260 pounds. He looked not more than 26. This big Negro was one 'bunch of joy,' always. Was his apparent happiness veneered, I asked myself, and forced just to show further contempt? No, I am sure it was due to other reasons. He was good natured as he was big, and his aim was to cheer and amuse his downhearted comrades who were less able to stand the strain.

"Johnson was an interesting story-teller as well as a good singer. When the prisoners asked their big mate to tell them a story, Johnson would cry out, 'All right, everybody keep quiet, and I will tell you all what happened to me night before last, while I was down town.' Then he would spin an interesting yarn of how he had been to town, and was having champagne suppers, and all the pretty girls falling in love with him. He would tell these stories so convincingly that more than one guard innocently inquired if Johnson had had a leave of absence lately. Johnson's friends claimed he was the champion liar of the world, but everybody encouraged him because he was so amusing.

"One day some colored folks came to sing and preach, and among them was a woman with a baby in her arms. Johnson wasn't much interested in the religious talk, but just as soon as he saw the baby he jumped up with his old time smile, stuck his big arm through the bars and begged the mother to let him hold the child only for a minute. This the woman did, and Johnson felt as though he had been given a privilege that was to be envied by a king. This was the only time I ever saw his eyes wet. He was telling the woman that he had a little baby brother at home.

"About ten days after the close of the trial, the colonel of the 19th Infantry, the judge advocate, and the chaplain appeared in the guardhouse. 'Sergeant,' said the colonel, 'have the men on this list brought up here and cuffed and shackled. Have two men come up at a time and chain them to each other.' As the sergeant started down the steps he winked at us, and whispered, 'The Death Detail.'

"The heavy voice of the sergeant broke the stillness of the prisoners' room: 'As I call the names off, I want you men to gather up all your belongings, including your blanket, then come front and center.' Everybody knew now that the names which were to be called were those of the doomed men.

"The prisoners soon came out with their things. As soon as they saw the handcuffs and shackles, they looked at each other with a sickly smile. They realized that they would have to face a firing squad or, worse still, a scaffold.

"The condemned men were marched to a room in one of the troops of the Sixth Cavalry. In the middle of the room was a little stove around which the men grouped in a circle, sitting on benches. About 11 o'clock that night the chaplain entered the room; his face was white as a sheet. He mentioned nothing relative to their sentence, but merely said he hoped each one had prepared to meet God. After reading from the Bible, and offering a short prayer, he told the men that he would come back later with a couple of colored ministers. Can you imagine how all this sounded to the prisoners who had not yet heard their sentence? During the chaplain's absence, someone suggested singing hymns. As the doomed men sang 'Nearer My God to Thee,' every listener's cheek was wet with tears.

"The chaplain returned the following night with two colored ministers. With a bowed head and in a low voice, he made known to them the verdict of the court-martial: 'You are all to be hanged tomorrow morning at the Slough at 7:17. You will leave here at 6 o'clock sharp. If any of you have any friends or relatives I could find nearby, I will gladly go and get them.' No one had any such friends. The men then asked if the chaplain would not intercede for them to see if they couldn't be shot instead of being hanged. But the chaplain shook his head, saying he had already made such a request but to no avail.

"The two colored preachers who were excellent singers tried to cheer the men by their songs. The saddest feature of the whole night was when they were singing the hymn 'Too Late.' The prisoners' faces were swollen for they had not slept a wink in four days. Most of them shut their eyes and their bodies were slumped down. As they shifted about on the bench, their chains rattled—a ghastly noise that seemed to fit the gloomy song they were singing.

"The next morning was cheerless and miserable. Five o'clock and pitch dark—no trace of a single star. The air was damp and cold, and a bleak wind which was blowing made the weather feel colder than if the thermometer had been at zero.

"At the stroke of 5:30, the lights of the huge army trucks began to pierce the darkness. Then came the clatter of horses' hoofs on the hard pavement—troops from the Sixth Cavalry who were to form a skirmish line a few hundred yards around the scaffold and to act as an extra guard going out. Every third or fourth rider carried a lantern. 'Fours right!—Halt!' rang the gruff command out of the darkness. As if the movement had been executed by a single horse, a straight line of cavalrymen were facing the barracks where the condemned men were confined.

"The night before the execution instructions were posted as to what each man was to do. I was to play the part of conductor. My duty was to help lead the doomed men up to the scaffold, carry them if necessary, then assist in putting the ropes about their necks.

"The jingle of the chains could now be heard, and the men were soon ready for their last ride. As soon as we started, the four men on my truck began to sing a hymn. After that Johnson, who was among them, made a speech. 'I want to thank you boys of C Company,' he said. 'You fellows didn't beat us, maybe like murderers ought to be treated, but we were treated like we were your brothers. If my thanks are worth anything to you men, I want to give it to you. If any of you ever go to France, I wish you all the luck in the world.' The men then stripped themselves of all their trinkets, and passed them out to the guards for souvenirs.

"Our gloomy procession was moving swiftly on toward the Slough. What a horrible ride it was! The headlight on the leading automobile at last found the scaffold, which had been put up that night. It was now day-break, but the grey, ugly dawn seemed only to give the scene added gloom. A gruesome spectacle it was—like a few acres borrowed from 'Dante's Hell.' Not far from the scaffold in the thick brushwood was a crackling bonfire. The sentries who had been up all night without a relief looked like Satan's favorite imps as they leaned over these little fires holding their fixed bayonets.

"The doomed men were shivering a little, but I think this was due more to the cold rather than fear. The unlucky 13 were lined up, not one making the slightest attempt to resist. The conductors took their places and the men for the last time heard the command, 'March!'

"Thirteen ropes dangled from the cross-beam of the scaffold, a chair in front of every rope, six on one side, seven on the other. As the ropes were being fastened about the men's necks, big Johnson's voice suddenly broke into a hymn—'Lord, I'm Comin' Home'—and the others joined him. The eyes of even the hardest of us were wet.

"A Catholic priest, a colored minister, and the Protestant chaplain of the 19th Infantry rose in succession and offered a few words of prayer. When they had finished, a major spoke to the doomed men, 'Just as soon as I give the command "Attention," I want you men to stand up.' 'Yes, sir,' they all smiled. The major raised his arms to horizontal position and in a loud voice shouted 'Attention.' Like the well trained soldiers they were, they sprang to their feet as one man, every one of them wearing a proud smile. 'Good-bye, C Company!' they called. The major lowered his hand to his side with a snap: this was the signal for the men to pull the rope to spring the trap. Away the chairs were jerked, down went the trap. . . . The men were executed at 7:17—the same precision with which everything is carried on in the Army.

"After they were taken down, each body was put into an expensive army casket, and carried about 50 yards from the scaffold where they were given a Christian burial. As I walked around the graves, it seemed impossible that the melodious voices of those men were stilled forever. Only a short while ago I heard them singing on the scaffold. That sad final hymn will always ring in my ears. . . . The whole thing was like a wild nightmare of a mad man. Such was my night at 'Hangman's Grove.' "

Dr. William Osler, having been invited to inspect a famous London hospital, was proudly shown about by several physicians and surgeons. Finally the charts were reached, and he looked them over carefully, observing the system of abbreviations: SF for scarlet fever, TB for tuberculosis, D for diphtheria, and so on. All diseases seemed to be pretty well under control except one indicated by the symbol GOK.

"I observe," said the famous doctor, "that you have a sweeping epidemic of GOK on your hands. This is a symbol not in common use in American medical circles; just what is GOK?"

"Oh!" one of his hosts lightly replied, "when *we* can't diagnose, God Only Knows."   —Quoted by Walter Neale in *Life of Ambrose Bierce*

An Appalachian guide, discussing his wife, remarked: "She has a very even temper—she is always mad."

Where there's a will there's a lawsuit.

He's in his anecdotage.

The stork is the bird with the long bill.

There isn't much to talk about at some parties until after one or two couples leave.

Defeat isn't bitter if you don't swallow it.

She knows how to give a man her own way.

Man is the only animal that can be skinned more than once.

Any girl can handle the beast in a man if she's cagey enough.

The trouble with a fat man is his daily doesn't.

Dignity is one thing that can't be preserved in alcohol.

Baby: An alimentary canal with a loud voice at one end and no responsibility at the other.

She's been in more laps than a napkin.

Her clothes are so designed that she is always seen in the best places.

The chairman replied in few appropriated words.

Child's definition: An adult is one who has stopped growing except in the middle.

I guess you'd call us friends—we have the same enemies.

It matters more what's in a woman's face than what's on it.

Gossips have a keen sense of rumor.

Give a husband enough rope . . . and he'll want to skip.

Mud thrown is ground lost.

Anger improves nothing except the arch of a cat's back.

Biology and our Future World

Condensed from Harper's Magazine

Julian Huxley

Eminent British biologist and writer

THE balance of nature is a very elaborate and very delicate system of checks and counterchecks. It is continually being altered as climates change and new organisms evolve. But in the past the alterations have been slow, whereas with the arrival of man their speed has been multiplied many fold.

Agriculture is the chief of man's efforts at the biological remodeling of nature. If we reflect that agriculture is less than a paltry 10,000 years old out of 300,000,000 years that green plants have been on earth, we begin to grasp something of the revolution wrought by this biological discovery.

But agriculture is, if you like, unnatural; it concentrates innumerable individuals as a single species—and always, of course, a particularly nutritious one—into serried ranks, while nature's method is to divide up the space among numerous competing or complementary kinds. Thus it constitutes not merely an opportunity but a veritable invitation to vegetable-feeding animals, of which the most difficult to control are the small, insinuating, and rapidly multiplying insects. And the better and more intensive the agriculture, the more obvious the invitation. Mile upon square mile of tender, well-weeded wheat or tea or cotton offers the optimum possibilities for the rapid multiplication of any species of insect which can take advantage of man's good nature toward his kind.

Finally, man's insatiable desire for rapid and easy transit has capped the trouble. By accident or intention, animals and plant species find their way along the trade routes to new countries. They are in a new environment, and in such circumstances the majority fail to gain a foothold at all; but a few find in the new circumstances a release instead of a hindrance, and multiply beyond measure.

Then it is up to the biologist to see what he can do. Sometimes, by

Copyright 1931, Harper & Bros., 49 E. 33 St., N. Y. C.

Selected from the October 1931 issue of The Reader's Digest

studying the pest in its original home, he can discover what are the other species that normally act as checks on its overmultiplication. Thus in Fiji, when the valuable coconut industry was threatened by a little moth—very beautiful, with violet wings—whose grubs devoured the leaves of the palm trees, biologists searched the remote corners of the Pacific for a parasitic fly. This fly quickly reduced the menace to the status of a minor nuisance. And in Australia, when prickly pear—first introduced into the country as pot cacti for lonely settlers' wives—increased so prodigiously that it was covering the land with impenetrable scrub at the rate of an acre a minute, biologists sent out a mixed team to fight it: a caterpillar to tunnel through the "leaves," a plant bug and a cochineal insect to suck its juices, and a mite to scarify its surface. These were the Four Anthropods of the prickly pear's Apocalypse; and the thickets are melting away under the combined attack.

One could multiply instances. How the sugar cane of Hawaii was saved from its weevil destroyers; how an attack is being launched upon the mealy-bugs that are such a pest to Kenya coffee by massed battalions of lady-birds. To cope with all the demands for anti-pest organisms a veritable industry has sprung up.

The difficulties of such work are far more severe when the pest is an old-established inhabitant of the country. Problems of this type are set for us by malaria, spread by indigenous mosquitoes; human sleeping sickness and nagana disease of cattle, transmitted by tsetse-flies; plague, dependent for its spread upon the ubiquitous rat. In some parts of Africa the issue is whether man or the fly shall dominate the country. Here the remedy seems to be to alter the whole environment. Most tsetse-flies live in bush country. They cannot exist either in quite open country or in cultivated land or in dense woodland or forest. So that wholesale clearing or afforestation may get rid of them.

That pests of this nature can cease to be serious is shown by the history of malaria and of plague. In various parts of Europe and America, these diseases, once serious, have wholly or virtually died out. And this has happened through a change in human environment and human habits. Take plague. Modern man builds better houses, clears away more garbage, segregates cases of infectious diseases, is less tolerant of dirt and parasites and, in fine, lives in such a way that his life is not in such close contact with that of rats. The result has been that rats have fewer chances of transmitting plague to man, and that the disease, if once transmitted, has less chance of spreading. With regard to malaria, agricultural drainage, cleanliness, and better general resistance have in

46

many cases done as much or more than deliberate anti-mosquito campaigns.

There is still another angle from which we can attack our problems. For instance, instead of trying to attack a pest by means of introducing enemies, or altering the environment, we can often deliberately breed stocks which shall be resistant to the attacks of the pest. Thus we can now produce relatively rust-proof wheat; and the Dutch have given us spectacular examples of what can be accomplished by crossing a high-yielding but disease-susceptible sugar cane with a related wild species which is disease-resistant and, in spite of the fact that the wild parent contains no trace of sugar, extracting from the cross after a few generations a disease-resistant plant with an exceptionally high yield of sugar.

Thus science offers the prospect of the most radical transformations of our environment. Cows or sheep, rubber-plants or beets represent from one aspect just so many living machines, designed to transform raw material into finished products available for man's use. And their machinery can be improved. Modern wheats yield several times as much per acre as unimproved varieties. Modern cows grow about twice as fast as the cattle kept by semi-savage tribes, and when they are grown produce two or three times as much milk in a year. This has thrown a new strain on the pastures; for if the cow eventually draws its nourishment out of the soil, and if the animal machine for utilizing grass is improved, the plant machine which is responsible for the first stage of the process, of working up raw materials out of earth and air, must be improved correspondingly. Accordingly research is trying to manufacture new breeds of grass which shall be as much more efficient than ordinary grass as a modern dairy beast is than the aboriginal cow.

These few examples must suffice to show the kind of control which man is just realizing he could exert over his environment. But they are enough to give us a new picture—the picture of a world controlled by man. It will never be fully controlled, but the future control of man will enormously exceed his present powers. The world will be parceled out into what is needed for crops, what for forests, what for gardens and parks and games, what for the preservation of wild nature; what grows on any part of the land's surface will grow there because of the conscious decision of man; and many kinds of animals and plants will owe not merely the fact that they are allowed to grow and exist, but their characteristics and their very nature, to human control.

My Conquest of Scarecrows

Condensed from "A Fortune to Share"

Vash Young

One of the most successful insurance salesmen in America, well known also for
his radio talks

I AM one of those lucky fellows who inherited a fortune. It came,
after years of poverty and reckless living, as result of a death I had
no cause to regret. The man who bequeathed riches to me was my
former self. He died of selfishness, pessimism, fear, worry, vain regrets,
envy. But this old Vash Young wasn't wholly bad, for he left me a great
store of courage, contentment, patience and freedom from harmful appetites. I took this inheritance out into business and it has made me
successful beyond my hopes.

As the old Vash Young I was an advertising salesman in New York,
where, despite turmoil and sourness inside me, I managed to make
a living while failing to make a life. I hadn't the faintest idea of how
happiness was to be achieved. Those were drinking, drifting days. Once
I sank so low that I planned to have a look at the next life, in the belief
that it could not be worse than this one.

But one day this idea popped into my mind:

"Suppose you owned a factory. Would you manufacture in it only
stuff you do not need? Would you deliberately operate it in such a way
as to make it harmful to you, the owner? Well, you do own a factory,
a thought factory. You are owner, superintendent, night watchman.
Nothing can come out of it except the products you yourself design.

"A thought factory! That's what you have inside you," I said to myself, "and you have turned it into a junk factory. Take a look at your
products. Fear, worry, impatience, anger, doubt. Your factory is a menace to yourself and a nuisance to others."

Obviously! Why hadn't I seen that before? My next step was to make
a list of qualities that seemed ever-enduring: Love, Courage, Cheerful-

Copyright 1931, Vash Young. "A Fortune to Share," published at $1.50 by The Bobbs-
Merrill Co., Indianapolis, is an extraordinary record of a remade life. No one reading
the book as a whole can fail to find repeated inspiration both in Mr. Young's philosophy and in his practical application of it to the problem of successful living.

Selected from July 1932 issue of The Reader's Digest

ness, Activity, Compassion, Friendliness, Generosity, Tolerance, Justice. Nine magic words! Night after night I sat alone with these words, fixing them in my consciousness, deciding what to do with them. *Reflect them in my conduct,* that's what I would do. They are all positive. They are dominant. They are stronger than their opposites. Live these words! That was the way out of the muck in which I had been groping.

First of all I decided I must do something to vanquish fear. All my life I had been afraid. The thing I feared most was loss of my job. I decided to call the bluff of this great bully, fear. I quit my job with nothing saved. Deliberately I brought about the condition I most feared.

There is no finer sensation in life than that which comes with victory over one's self. The morning after I found myself jobless, with less than $100 and with a wife and daughter trusting me to care for them, I had not one feeling of fear—only elation, romance, joy at a new start in a new world.

I started from scratch, as an insurance salesman, the most highly competitive of occupations. I had to stop thinking about myself, forget the past, leave the future to care for itself and concentrate on today. Doubts tried to creep into my mind, but every time a negative thought came I thrust it out of my consciousness and thought of something worth while. This is a habit any one can acquire. Try it. At first the unwholesome thoughts will struggle, but they are not strong enough to win.

For a time my household was hard up, but we were happier than we had ever been before, for we were fighting and winning a series of battles. One of my first fights was to cut out all habits which seemed to be harmful. I found that liquor, coffee, tea and tobacco all could be dispensed with, so within the space of a single day I cut these things out of my life. It wasn't easy. It took reason and understanding to win the day. Dominion over these habits was a great victory for me. A great victory almost always makes subsequent victories easy.

A second battle was to get rid of self-centeredness. For there came a time when our condition was desperate, and I wavered and had to check myself sharply. "When you are keenly conscious of your own needs, do something for somebody else!" I demanded. So every Sunday for the next year I went to a hospital on the East Side of New York and sang for the crippled children there. Before that year was over, I had money. By refusing to put money first I had hit on a profitable program.

A third fight was my determination never to undertake any business venture if my happiness would be in the least disturbed in case it failed.

When my dominion over disappointment was entrenched, I still had a bad temper to lick. A trivial adventure did that and was worth millions to me in happiness. After working very late one night, I dived into the subway, dog tired, eager to be in bed. The guard of a waiting train slammed the door in my face. There would not be another for 15 minutes. I felt hot anger sweep over me. I started to yell at the guard, but then I stopped. Why burn up what little energy I had left? Looking around, I saw a woman leaving the station with a baby and a suitcase. I asked if I could help her, took her suitcase, hailed a taxicab, drove her to her destination. Then I started home, two hours after I had missed the subway train. My fatigue was gone and I was very happy. I had put myself through a course of discipline by doing something for somebody else.

The subject of fear is a favorite of mine. Fear is the greatest enemy of most persons. Every friend I have has lost something because of fear. Read biographies and you encounter frequent accounts of combats with fear, for men about whom biographies are written usually are those who overcome this emotion. Few persons go through life without at least one big chance. The fact that so many do not grasp it is due more often to fear than to any other thing. "Never strike a sail to fear," says Emerson, and every man who has occupied a commanding position has said the same.

No man has ever had a harder fight against fear than I had. There is not a doubt nor a dread nor a sick sensation I have not suffered. Most people are afraid of something, but I was afraid of almost everything, including mice, thunderstorms, teachers, physical encounters. In my first days as a salesman I often became so nauseated as I contemplated my next calls that I lost my food in the gutter. Literally that is true. Not once, but time after time, due always to fear. I have prayed—how I have prayed!—that my prospects would be out of the office when I got there.

But one day I stopped and spoke to myself. "You miserable coward!" I said. "You set out to do a job and you crawl out on it. Go and see those men!" And I called on every one of the men I had dreaded to call on, I had delightful talks with some of them and went home happy.

When I was a boy farmers used scarecrows in their fields. Timid birds, seeing the flapping of an old coat on crossed sticks, would fly away, but now and then a wiser bird would come down and enjoy a feast, using the scarecrow as a perch. Since I became tired of being a fool, it has occurred to me time and again that the fears of life are nothing more than scarecrows. Realization of this is the heart of the fortune I inherited.

This inheritance, as I have said, requires that I do everything possible for my fellow humans. I try. I have made it a rule these past ten successful years to devote less than half of my time to my own affairs. A considerable part of my happiness comes from these extra-official duties. I give each Saturday to people who are in trouble. The fortune which I share with people who come to me on "Trouble Day" is really my religion. This is what I think religion is:

It is saying gratefully in the morning, "Thank you, God, for what I have," instead of, "Please give me a lot more."

It is trying to make somebody happier for the day before leaving home.

It is pausing long enough in the morning to telephone to some friend who may need a word of encouragement. In doing this you develop the habit of thinking more of others than of yourself. The results will surprise you. As an insurance salesman, for instance, my plans differ radically from the standard plan of selling. I always submit a policy smaller than I think the man should take out, and let him raise it. That makes him feel comfortable. My idea always is to make a man on whom I call glad that I came. This I do as a matter of ethics. It is just a fine break of life that in some cases business follows in the wake of considerate conduct.

Again, religion to me is planning for the day more constructive work than we can possibly do. It is the exercise of constant dominion over harmful emotions and false appetites. It is telling other people of things they have done which merit praise. It is development of the "giving" habit instead of the "getting" habit.

Finally, religion to me is living now, on this earth, as nearly as possible the life we imagine the next one to be. Selfishness, pride, greed, envy, fear, worry, hate and anger undoubtedly do not exist in the heavenly state. Heaven is unquestionably made up of such positive qualities as love, courage, cheerfulness, generosity. We can be in Heaven right here on earth by *living* these qualities. Life becomes almost automatic once you have tapped their sources of strength. It is silly for a poor mortal to buck the stream of life. I have sought out its current and have sought to flow with it. That stream is impelled by those positive qualities, and it is the fortune they have brought me that I'd like to share with all.

The Other Half of Helen Keller

Condensed from "Anne Sullivan Macy: The Story Behind Helen Keller"

Nella Braddy

NEARLY EVERYONE remembers that a girl by the name of Annie Sullivan went to Alabama many years ago and set free the spirit of a child who was blind, deaf, and dumb. The devotion of these 46 years is not so well known. Many people have asked for the story of her life, and Anne Sullivan Macy has pointed to Helen Keller as all the biography she desires. But it is time now to talk about "Teacher"—Helen never called her anything else.

Because of the squalor into which she was born at Feeding Hills, Mass., Annie developed a destructive inflammation of the eyes so early that the first words she can remember were: "She would be so pretty if it were not for her eyes." It was not only Annie's eyes that distressed her mother, Annie was passionately rebellious in the way a child is likely to be who is surrounded by unhappiness. She can remember some of her tantrums. Once in anger she rocked her little sister clear out of her cradle and gave her a cruel scar on her forehead. One winter afternoon, a neighbor came with a little girl in white shoes and white mittens, soft like rabbits. Annie wanted the white mittens intensely, but the neighbor had brought red mittens for her. "I don't want them," she cried and threw them into the fire.

When her mother died nobody wanted half-blind Annie nor her little brother, Jimmie, who was born with a tubercular hip. There was only one place where they could be sent, the Tewksbury poorhouse. Their ward was filled with old women, misshapen, diseased, and dying. "Very much of what I remember about Tewksbury," she says, "is in-

Copyright 1933, Nella Braddy Henney, and reprinted by permission of Doubleday, Doran & Co., Inc.

Selected from December 1933 issue of The Reader's Digest

decent, cruel, and gruesome in the light of grown-up experience, but it was all the life I knew." And then Jimmie died. "I sat down between my bed and his empty bed, and I longed desperately to die. I believe very few children have ever been so completely left alone as I was. I felt that I was the only thing that was alive in the world."

Two operations in Tewksbury apparently had done nothing for her sight, and finally she was taken to the city infirmary in Boston. But when the doctors there were through with her, the eyes were still so blurred that she could be classified in public records only as blind.

The old women at the almshouse had told Annie that the most famous of schools where blind children could be taught to read and write was only 20 miles away. "I want to go to that school," she begged; and at last, without a toothbrush, petticoat, hat, or coat, she entered the Perkins Institution. That night, for the first time in her life, she slept in a nightgown. She was 14 years old; Helen Keller was 3 months old.

At Perkins, the teachers had a hard time finding a place for her. Mat weaving was the orthodox starting point but she couldn't weave and cursed the mat. The teachers tried her somewhere else and everywhere she went it was the same. Bewildered, rebellious, she fought her way through classes accepting nothing on the authority of the teachers. "My mind was a question mark, my heart a frustration," she says. The following summer a young doctor became interested in her eyes and after two operations, 12 months apart, the curtain was lifted. Delirious with her new powers, she swept into books and newspapers, stealing them from the teachers. In 1886 she was graduated from Perkins, valedictorian of her class of eight.

In the meantime, in Tuscumbia, Ala., a serious illness had left Helen Keller, then 19 months old, irrevocably blind, deaf, and dumb. Day after day, her mother watched the little girl slipping from her, yet trying, even as she herself was trying, to hold the few strands of communication left. All day long the little animal tugged at her mother's skirts, strong, tireless, quick tempered, and wilful. "You ought to put her away," said Helen's uncle, "she is mentally defective." But an aunt kept saying: "This child has more sense than all the Kellers, if there is ever any way to reach her mind." Mrs. Keller never gave up hope that there would be a way. She had read in Dickens' *American Notes* of his visit to the Perkins Institution 40 years before and thought the child could be taught. Her husband finally found that the Perkins Institution was still in existence and wrote its director. So in March, 1887, Annie Sullivan arrived in Tuscumbia.

It was Annie's plan to move slowly, first winning Helen's love. She learned the following day that Helen had always done exactly as she pleased and intended to keep on. Sometimes it was impossible for days to comb her hair; force was necessary to button her shoes or wash her face. Annie recognized immediately that her biggest problem was to get Helen under some kind of control without breaking her spirit. This could not be done while Helen was with her family, none of whom could bear to see the child punished. Mrs. Keller finally consented to their living in a little annex near the Keller homestead where the family visited them every day. The experiment began badly. Helen was homesick and would have nothing to do with Annie. Helen's father looked through the window one morning at ten o'clock and saw Helen sitting on the floor, still in her nightgown, the picture of stubbornness and despair. With tears in his eyes he said: "I've a good mind to send that Yankee girl back to Boston," but he was dissuaded.

Two weeks later, Annie wrote: "My heart is singing for joy. The little savage has learned her first lesson in obedience, and finds the yoke easy. It remains my pleasant task to direct and mould the intelligence that is beginning to stir in the child-soul." By touching objects and by finger movements into Helen's hand, Annie began teaching the child to spell. "One day we went to the pump house. I made Helen hold her mug under the spout while I pumped. As the cold water gushed forth, I spelled 'w-a-t-e-r' several times. All the way back to the house she was highly excited, and learned the name of every object she touched. In a few hours she had added 30 new words to her vocabulary." If this was a momentous day for Helen, it was no less so for her teacher, for that night Helen for the first time of her own accord, snuggled into bed with her and kissed her. The loneliness that had tracked Annie since Jimmie's death was gone now. "I thought my heart would burst, it was so full of joy," she said.

Three months after her arrival in Tuscumbia, she wrote: "I know that Helen has remarkable powers, and I believe that I shall be able to develop and mould them. She is no ordinary child and people's interest in her education will be no ordinary interest; but she shall not be transformed into a prodigy if I can help it." How the Kellers felt they told Annie at Christmas, when the happy, intelligent face of their child brought keenly to memory the sad Christmases of the four preceding years.

"I thank God every day for sending you to us," cried Mrs. Keller; Captain Keller took her hand but could not speak.

54

When Annie felt unequal to a situation she turned for help to the person who seemed best equipped in all the world to carry her through. In the case of Helen's voice she took her to Miss Sara Fuller of the Horace Mann School for the Deaf, in Boston. At the end of 11 lessons Helen was able to say haltingly: "I-am-not-dumb-now." For 40 years Annie and Helen labored incessantly with Helen's voice and if Annie had been able to devote her entire time to teaching Helen to speak, the results might have been more satisfying. But she and Helen both realized that to have something to say was more important than to have a beautiful way of saying it.

Annie never let pity blind her common sense. She demanded of Helen what she would have demanded of a seeing and hearing girl, more in fact, for it took Helen twice as long to prepare her lessons. To this Helen owes the fact that she has been accepted on equal terms by the seeing and hearing, and this is the greatest pride of her life. Annie never emphasized Helen's dependence upon her, but Mark Twain once wrote Helen: "You are a wonderful creature—you and your other half together—Miss Sullivan, I mean, for it took the pair of you to make a complete and perfect whole."

When Annie consented to marry John Macy in 1905, she reconsidered so many times that Mr. Macy threatened to print "Subject to change without notice" on the wedding invitations. There were many arguments against the marriage: Helen must come first, Helen was her child, her life. So, in a house jointly owned, the Macys and Helen continued to live. Except for absences of a few weeks, Annie has been separated from Helen but twice in 46 years. In 1916 when Mrs. Macy was ill in Porto Rico, Helen wrote her: "How alone and unprepared I feel! Thirty years ago you, a young girl alone in the world, handicapped by imperfect vision and want of experience, came and opened life's shut portal and let in joy, hope, knowledge, and friendship."

In 1930, Mr. Walter Pitkin listed the living Americans who, in his opinion, had achieved most. Helen Keller's name was in the first group which included only 4 names. Mrs. Macy, with 10 others, was in the second, but Mr. Pitkin said: "A strong case might be put up in favor of promoting this extraordinary woman to the first group."

Temple University invited Helen and Mrs. Macy to receive the degree of Doctor of Humane Letters in 1931. Helen accepted, but Mrs. Macy wrote: "I cannot conscientiously receive the degree. I do not consider my education commensurate." But they wanted her to have the degree. Still she was firm. In the Temple auditorium, after the other speakers had showered praise upon Helen, Dr. A. Edward Newton asked all in the audience who felt that the degree should be conferred upon Mrs. Macy, by force, if necessary, to rise. Only one person remained seated, and that was Anne Sullivan Macy. When she returned a year later to receive that degree, reporters clustered around Helen. There was only one reporter who talked with Mrs. Macy. "Even at my coronation Helen is queen," she said proudly.

You will find Anne Sullivan Macy today in Forest Hills, Long Island, with her dogs. There have always been dogs in her life. The most notable was a Great Dane whom—it is difficult to make people credit this—she taught to say: "Ma-ma." The dog also asked for water by pronouncing: "Wah-ter." Many reporters who saw and heard this necromancy felt that they had enough on their hands in making readers believe in Helen without adding the story of the dog.

Mrs. Macy is now nearly 70 and there is only a dim flicker of sight left; but the old fires still burn high. Not many months ago, friends, with the greatest difficulty, persuaded her that it was not a sane and practical plan to have another pupil, to make a little neglected deaf and blind child a member of her household. She still likes the rich warm tide of life where it strikes the rapids, not where it runs smooth. She is anchored to two great rocks of faith; one is that obstinate belief in people which no number of disappointments have ever been able to kill; and the other is Helen.

Could Annie Sullivan have done better by the world and in the world if she had scattered her abilities? She thinks not. If Helen Keller had been nothing more than a good broom-maker, Annie Sullivan would have concentrated on broom-making. She would not have stayed with Helen these 46 years; but one may safely say that she would not have left until she had taught her to be the best blind broom-maker in the world.

Beautiful young people are accidents of nature. But beautiful old people are works of art.
—Marjorie Barstow Greenbie, Be Your Age (Stackpole)

The Doctor of Lennox

By
A. J. Cronin

Author of "The Stars Look Down," "The Citadel," etc.

THE MOST unforgettable character I ever met? To my surprise I find myself thinking, not of some famous statesman, soldier or tycoon, but of a simple soul who had no wish to dominate an empire, but set out instead to conquer circumstance—and himself.

I first knew him as a boy, small, insignificant and poor, who hung on to us, so to speak, by the skin of his teeth—barely accepted by the select band of adventurous youths of which I was one in my native Scottish town of Levenford.

If he were in any way remarkable, it was through his defects. He was quite comically lame, one leg being so much shorter than the other that he was obliged to wear a boot with a sole six inches thick. To see him run, saving his bad leg, his undersized form tense and limping, the sweat breaking out on his eager face, well—Chisholm, the minister's son, acknowledged wit of our band, hit the nail on the head when he dubbed him Dot-and-Carry. It was shortened subsequently to Carry. "Look out," someone would shout, "here comes Carry. Let's get away before he tags on to us." And off we would dart, to the swimming pool or the woods, with Carry, dotting along, cheerful and unprotesting, in our wake.

That was his quality, a shy, a smiling cheerfulness—and how we mocked it! To us, Carry was an oddity. His clothes, though carefully patched and mended, were terrible. Socially he was almost beyond the

57

pale. His mother, a gaunt little widow of a drunken loafer, supported herself and her son by scrubbing out sundry shops. Again Chisholm epitomized the jest with his classic epigram, "Carry's mother takes in stairs to wash."

Carry supplemented the family income by rising at five o'clock every morning to deliver milk. This long milk round sometimes made him late for school. Glancing down the arches of the years, I can still see a small lame boy, hot and trembling, in the middle of the classroom floor, while the master, a sadistic brute, drew titters with his shafts.

"Well, well . . . can it be possible ye're late again?"

"Y-y-yes, sir."

"And where has your lordship been? Taking breakfast with the provost no doubt?"

"N-n-n-n-"

At such moments of crisis Carry had a stammer which rose and tortured him. He could not articulate another syllable. And the class, reading permission in the master's grim smile, dissolved in roars of mirth.

If Carry had been clever, all might have been well for him. In Scotland everything is forgiven the brilliant "lad o' pairts." But though Carry did well enough at his books, oral examinations were to him the crack of doom.

There was heartburning in this fact for Carry's mother. She longed for her son to excel, and to excel in one especial field. Poor, humble, despised, she nourished in her fiercely religious soul a fervent ambition. She desired to see her son an ordained minister of the Church of Scotland. Sublime folly! But Carry's mother had sworn to achieve the miracle or die!

Carry much preferred the open countryside to a stuffy prayer meeting. He loved the woods and moors and the wild things that lived there— was never happier than when tending some sick or maimed creature picked up on his wanderings. He had a most uncanny knack of healing. In fact, Carry had a tremendous longing to be a doctor.

But obedience was inherent in his gentle nature, and when he left school it was to enter college as a student of divinity. Heaven knows how they managed. His mother scrimped and saved, her figure grew more gaunt, but in her deep-set eye there glowed unquenchable fire. Carry himself, though his heart was not in what he did, worked like a hero.

And so it happened, quicker than might have been imagined, that Carry was duly licensed at the age of 24 in the cure of souls according to the Kirk of Scotland. Locally there was great interest in the prodigy of the scrubwoman's son turned parson. He was proposed for the parish church assistantship and named to preach a trial sermon.

A full congregation assembled to see "what was in the young meenister." And Carry, who for weeks past had rehearsed his sermon, ascended the pulpit feeling himself word-perfect. He began to speak in an earnest voice and for a few moments he went well enough. Then all at once he became conscious of those rows and rows of upturned faces, of his mother dressed in her best in a front pew, her eyes fixed rapturously upon him. A paralyzing shiver of self-distrust swept over him. He hesitated, lost the thread of his ideas and began to stammer. Once that frightful impotence of speech had gripped him he was lost. He labored on pitifully, but while he struggled for the words he saw the restlessness, the significant smiles; heard even a faint titter. And then again he saw his mother's face, and broke down completely. There was a long and awful pause, then falteringly Carry drew the service to a close by announcing the hymn.

Within the hour, when Carry's mother reached home, she was mercifully taken by an apoplectic seizure. She never spoke again.

The funeral over, Carry disappeared from Levenford. No one knew or cared where he went. He was stigmatized, branded contemptuously for life, a failure. When some years later news reached me that he was teaching in a wretched school in a mining district, I thought of him for a moment, with a kind of shamefaced sorrow, as a despairing soul, a man predestined for disaster. But I soon forgot him.

I was working in Edinburgh when Chisholm, now first assistant to the Regius Professor of Anatomy there, dropped into my rooms one evening. "You'll never guess," he grinned, "who's dissecting in my department. None other than our boyhood friend, Dot-and-Carry."

Carry it was. Carry, at nearly 30 years of age, starting out to be a doctor! A strange figure he made, with his shabby suit, his limp and stoop, among the gay young bucks who were his fellow students. No one ever spoke to him. He occupied a room in a poor district, cooked his own meals, husbanded the slender savings from his teacher's pittance. I saw something of his struggle for the next two years. His age, appearance, and traitorous stammer hampered him. But he went plodding indefatigably on, refusing to admit defeat, the old dogged cheerfulness and hopeful courage still in his eyes.

Time marched on. Five years and more. I found myself in London, and had long since again lost touch with Carry. But I saw much of

Chisholm, whose good looks and glib tongue had destined him for political honors. He was now indeed a Member of Parliament and a junior minister into the bargain. In May of 1934 I went with him for a fishing holiday at Lennox in the Highlands. The food at our inn was vile and the landlady a scrawny shrew. It was something of a satisfaction when, two days after our arrival, she slipped on the taproom floor and damaged her kneecap. Perfunctorily, we two renegades from the healing art offered our assistance. But the dame would have none of us. No one would suit but her own village doctor, of whose canny skill and notable achievements she drew an enthusiastic picture that made Chisholm glance at me and smile.

An hour later the practitioner arrived, black bag in hand, with all the quick assurance of a busy man. In no time he had silenced the patient with a reassuring word and reduced the dislocation with a sure, deft touch. Only then did he turn toward us.

"My God!" exclaimed Chisholm, under his breath. "Carry!"

Yes, Carry it was. But not the shy, shabby, stammering Carry of old. He had the quietly confident air of a man established and secure. In a flash of recognition he greeted us warmly, and pressed us to come to supper at his home. Meanwhile, he had an urgent case to attend.

It was with an odd expectancy, half excitement and half lingering misgiving, that we entered the village doctor's house that evening. What a shock to find that Carry had a wife! Yet it was so. She welcomed us, fresh and pretty as her own countryside. Since the doctor (she gave the title with a naïve reverence) was still engaged in his surgery, she took us upstairs to see the children. Two red-cheeked girls and a little boy, already asleep. Surprise made us mute.

Downstairs, Carry joined us with two other guests. Now, at his own table, he was a man poised and serene, holding his place as host with quiet dignity. His friends, both men of substance, treated him with deference. Less from what he said than what was said by others we gathered the facts. His practice was wide and scattered. His patients were country folk, canny, silent, hard to know. Yet somehow he had won them. Now as he went through a village the women would run to him, babe in arms, to consult him in the roadway. Such times he never bothered about fees. More than enough came his way, and at New Year there was always a string of presents on his doorstep, a brace of ducks, a goose, a clutch of new-laid eggs, in handsome settlement for some quite forgotten service.

But there were other tales—of midnight vigils when in some humble home the battle for a human life was waged: a child, choking with diphtheria, a plowman stricken with pneumonia, a shepherd's wife in painful labor, all to be sustained, comforted, exhorted, brought back haltingly, their hands in his, from the shadows.

The doctor was a force now, permeating the whole countryside, wise and gentle, blending the best of science and nature, unsparing, undemanding, loving this work he had been born to do, conscious of the place that he had won in the affections of the people, a man who had refused defeat and won through to victory at last.

Late that night as we left the doctor's house and trudged through the darkness, silence fell between Chisholm and myself. Then, as with an effort, he declared:

"It looks as though the little man has found himself at last."

Something patronizing in the remark jarred me. I could not resist a quick reply.

"Which would you rather be, Chisholm—yourself, or the doctor of Lennox?"

"Confound you," he muttered. "Don't you know?"

A letter from a family which had to be poor, but refused to be impoverished—

Condensed from The Atlantic Monthly

DEAREST ELIZABETH,

You say in your letter, "Do not sympathize—just tell me what you did to meet a similar emergency." Even though you forbid it, I do sympathize. This last blow is altogether merciless because it comes when you believed the worst really was over. But, merciless or not, the emergency has to be faced. So I am opening wide the book of my experience. . . .

The first thing I did was to call the children into conference. I felt that our only hope for survival lay in complete coöperation. I began by reminding them that their father's record of achievement is such that we all have justifiable reason to be proud. I assured them that eventually a man of his ability must find his place in the economic world. I warned them, however, that I did not know how long this readjustment might take. Meanwhile we were going right on being proud of him and having faith in him.

Then I did a very prideful thing: I got out the history of their father's family and traced the part these men and women, whose name they bear, had played in developing this country. I said, "You see, once upon a time this country had need for men and women like you. That need may come again. Consequently, I am not going to allow you to be wasted."

I told them that history was full of periods when just to survive was triumph. (And this, Elizabeth, is my answer to your question, "If I can offer my children nothing but a bare existence, why bother with that at all?") I admitted that, for the present, adequate shelter, the simplest of food, and something in the way of clothes were the very most we could do for them.

I was almost brutally honest; I had to be. If I went about singing,

> Just around the corner
> There's a rainbow in the sky . . .

Copyright 1934, The Atlantic Monthly Co., 8 Arlington St., Boston, Mass.
(The Atlantic Monthly, July, '34)

Selected from September 1934 issue of The Reader's Digest

and that rainbow failed to appear, I should no longer have the confidence of my children. I *had* to have that if I was to see them through. I told them that the fight for survival was always a grim business, but that we were not going to be a bit grim about it. We were going to be the jolliest soldiers that were ever put through a forced march.

I warned them that each of us would have to develop great respect for a penny, but that we did not have to worship it. To me that seems one of the most unpleasant characteristics of so many people of little means; they overestimate the importance of money and underestimate the value of everything else.

We were going to be poor, but we did not have to become impoverished because we were still rich in so much that made life worth living. "You children," I told them, "have more than average health and intelligence. There has always been harmony in your home and there always will be. You have beautiful memories of places, and your lives have touched interesting and worth-while people. You have the best of books and they are friends who will stand by you. You have a good radio which brings you the best in music and splendid bits of drama. These are your riches; with them you will have to be content for the present."

Then I told each one how I thought he was particularly well adapted to go through this adjustment period and where I thought he might prove vulnerable. I went even further and told them just where I anticipated trouble in myself. "No crisis has ever yet found me lacking in courage, but I am not certain that I have enough of the dogged, persistent kind of courage which can hold out day after day. If I am lacking in that, you children will have to bear with me and help me in every way you can while I am learning to develop it. Our success in this new venture will be determined largely by the sympathy, understanding and tenderness we display toward each other."

It was a big order I was giving my children, much too large to hope to fill completely. But they have come so close to filling it that our pride in them is colossal. My children know more about courage, steadfastness and self-control than many people learn in a lifetime. Besides that, they have gone far in tolerance and understanding. Never will they say as their mother used to do, "how in the world did people like that ever get into such a jam?" because they know too much about "jams" to be impatient with anybody who is in one. They have taken big strides in the art of coöperation, no mean art to master. They have developed perspective, for, when one fixes his eyes upon the mountains the molehills over which he stumbles slip by unnoticed.

As a family we have become rank opportunists. Our faith in "to-morrow" has been so often betrayed that we put no stock in it whatso-ever. Today is here. So we set out to squeeze every last drop of pleasure and fun out of each day. When the plate goes suddenly bare, one learns to appreciate the little that is left or else one spends his life in drooping melancholy. We, as a family, do not choose to droop.

In some ways it is easier to have a good time than ever before because we are so eager for happiness and because we are no longer weighed down with the appurtenances of nice living. For example, picnics used to be the bane of my existence because there was so much to prepare and pack. Now, we take a meat pie out of the oven, put a couple of bottles of milk and a few apples into a basket, and wander down to the creek to eat.

Still, I miss nice living, and so will you. You will miss much else besides, such as folks that are stimulating, places that are new and different. You'll miss comfort and luxury, and, above all, you will miss the future. Until I become an opportunist I never realized how much time I spent dreaming of the children's future. I wanted to do so much for them, especially for the girls—one feels that a man-child can get by somehow, if he has the proper stuff in him. The change has been difficult but I am a bit reconciled to it.

A few weeks ago we were invited to a dinner party. One of the guests was a girl who impressed me more than any stranger ever has. She was lovely to look at, beautifully poised, her voice was charming, she had the "grand manner" and yet was delightfully gracious. I kept thinking, "Surely *this* girl has had many advantages!" But when I inquired I found that her education had been confined to high school and a very short business course. This experience reminded me that the word "educate" means to lead forth, and if my daughters have in themselves something worth while, it is possible that they will become true gentlewomen anyway. I pass that thought on because I know that your darkest hours will come when you allow yourself to contrast what you *can* do for your children with what you had intended to do.

You and I, Elizabeth, have been dealt a no-honor hand, but I think that we are able to take some tricks yet. When or how I do not know. But I am not ready to throw down my hand in disgust, and I feel very confident that, when you have had a little longer to accustom yourself to your new circumstances, you will want to go on playing the hand, too.

MARY

—And Sudden Death

By

J. C. Furnas

Like the gruesome spectacle of a bad automobile accident itself, the realistic details of this article will nauseate some readers. Those who find themselves thus affected at the outset are cautioned against reading the article in its entirety, since there is no letdown in the author's outspoken treatment of sickening facts.

PUBLICIZING the total of motoring injuries—almost a million in *one year*, with 36,000 deaths—never gets to first base in jarring the motorist into a realization of the appalling risks of motoring. He does not translate dry statistics into a reality of blood and agony.

Figures exclude the pain and horror of savage mutilation—which means they leave out the point. They need to be brought closer home. A passing look at a bad smash or the news that a fellow you had lunch with last week is in a hospital with a broken back will make any driver but a born fool slow down at least temporarily. But what is needed is a vivid and *sustained* realization that every time you step on the throttle, death gets in beside you, hopefully waiting for his chance. That single horrible accident you may have witnessed is no isolated horror. That sort of thing happens every hour of the day, everywhere in the United States. If you really felt *that*, perhaps the stickful of type in Monday's paper recording that a total of 29 local citizens were killed in week-end crashes would rate something more than a perfunctory tut-tut as you turn back to the sports page.

An enterprising judge now and again sentences reckless drivers to tour the accident end of a city morgue. But even a mangled body on a slab, waxily portraying the consequences of bad motoring judgment,

Selected from August 1935 issue of The Reader's Digest

isn't a patch on the scene of the accident itself. No artist working on a safety poster would dare depict that in full detail.

That picture would have to include motion-picture and sound effects, too—the flopping, pointless efforts of the injured to stand up; the queer, grunting noises; the steady, panting groaning of a human being with pain creeping up on him as the shock wears off. It should portray the slack expression on the face of a man, drugged with shock, staring at the Z-twist in his broken leg, the insane crumpled effect of a child's body after its bones are crushed inward, a realistic portrait of an hysterical woman with her screaming mouth opening a hole in the bloody drip that fills her eyes and runs off her chin. Minor details would include the raw ends of bones protruding through flesh in compound fractures, and the dark red, oozing surfaces where clothes and skin were flayed off at once.

Those are all standard, every-day sequels to the modern passion for going places in a hurry and taking a chance or two by the way. If ghosts could be put to a useful purpose, every bad stretch of road in the United States would greet the oncoming motorist with groans and screams and the educational spectacle of ten or a dozen corpses, all sizes, sexes and ages, lying horribly still on the bloody grass.

Last year a state trooper of my acquaintance stopped a big red Hispano for speeding. Papa was obviously a responsible person, obviously set for a pleasant week-end with his family—so the officer cut into papa's well-bred expostulations: "I'll let you off this time, but if you keep on this way, you won't last long. Get going—but take it easier." Later a passing motorist hailed the trooper and asked if the red Hispano had got a ticket. "No," said the trooper, "I hated to spoil their party." "Too bad you didn't," said the motorist, "I saw you stop them—and then I passed that car again 50 miles up the line. It still makes me feel sick at my stomach. The car was all folded up like an accordion—the color was about all there was left. They were all dead but one of the kids—and he wasn't going to live to the hospital."

Maybe it will make you sick at your stomach, too. But unless you're a heavy-footed incurable, a good look at the picture the artist wouldn't dare paint, a first-hand acquaintance with the results of mixing gasoline

with speed and bad judgment, ought to be well worth your while. I can't help it if the facts are revolting. If you have the nerve to drive fast and take chances, you ought to have the nerve to take the appropriate cure.

You can't ride an ambulance or watch the doctor working on the victim in the hospital, but you can read.

The automobile is treacherous, just as a cat is. It is tragically difficult to realize that it can become the deadliest missile. As enthusiasts tell you, it makes 65 feel like nothing at all. But 65 an hour is 100 feet a second, a speed which puts a viciously unjustified responsibility on brakes and human reflexes, and can instantly turn this docile luxury into a mad bull elephant.

Collision, turnover or sideswipe, each type of accident produces either a shattering dead stop or a crashing change of direction—and, since the occupant—meaning you—continues in the old direction at the original speed, every surface and angle of the car's interior immediately becomes a battering, tearing projectile, aimed squarely at you—inescapable. There is no bracing yourself against these imperative laws of momentum.

It's like going over Niagara Falls in a steel barrel full of railroad spikes. The best thing that can happen to you—and one of the rarer things—is to be thrown out as the doors spring open, so you have only the ground to reckon with. True, you strike with as much force as if you had been thrown from the *Twentieth Century* at top speed. But at least you are spared the lethal array of gleaming metal knobs and edges and glass inside the car.

Anything can happen in that split second of crash, even those lucky escapes you hear about. People have dived through windshields and come out with only superficial scratches. They have run cars together head on, reducing both to twisted junk, and been found unhurt and arguing bitterly two minutes afterward. But death was there just the same—he was only exercising his privilege of being erratic. This spring a wrecking crew pried the door off a car which had been overturned down an embankment and out stepped the driver with only a scratch on his cheek. But his mother was still inside, a splinter of wood from the top driven four inches into her brain as a result of son's taking a greasy curve a little too fast. No blood—no horribly twisted bones—just a gray-haired corpse still clutching her pocketbook in her lap as she had clutched it when she felt the car leave the road.

On that same curve a month later, a light touring car crashed a tree. In the middle of the front seat they found a nine-months-old baby surrounded by broken glass and yet absolutely unhurt. A fine practical joke on death—but spoiled by the baby's parents, still sitting on each side of him, instantly killed by shattering their skulls on the dashboard.

If you customarily pass without clear vision a long way ahead, make sure that every member of the party carries identification papers—it's difficult to identify a body with its whole face bashed in or torn off. The driver is death's favorite target. If the steering wheel holds together it ruptures his liver or spleen so he bleeds to death internally. Or, if the steering wheel breaks off, the matter is settled instantly by the steering column's plunging through his abdomen.

By no means do all head-on collisions occur on curves. The modern death-trap is likely to be a straight stretch with three lanes of traffic—like the notorious Astor Flats on the Albany Post Road where there have been as many as 27 fatalities in one summer month. This sudden vision of broad, straight road tempts many an ordinarily sensible driver into passing the man ahead. Simultaneously a driver coming the other way swings out at high speed. At the last moment each tries to get into line again, but the gaps are closed. As the cars in line are forced into the ditch to capsize or crash fences, the passers meet, almost head on, in a swirling, grinding smash that sends them caroming obliquely into the others.

A trooper described such an accident—five cars in one mess, seven killed on the spot, two dead on the way to the hospital, two more dead in the long run. He remembered it far more vividly than he wanted to—the quick way the doctor turned away from a dead man to check up on a woman with a broken back; the three bodies out of one car so soaked with oil from the crank-case that they looked like wet brown cigars and not human at all; a man, walking around and babbling to himself, oblivious of the dead and dying, even oblivious of the dagger-like sliver of steel that stuck out of his streaming wrist; a pretty girl with her forehead laid open, trying hopelessly to crawl out of a ditch in spite of her smashed hip. A first-class massacre of that sort is only a question of scale and numbers—seven corpses are no deader than one. Each shattered man, woman or child who went to make up the 36,000 corpses chalked up last year had to die a personal death.

A car careening and rolling down a bank, battering and smashing its occupants every inch of the way, can wrap itself so thoroughly around a tree that front and rear bumpers interlock, requiring an acetylene torch to cut them apart. In a recent case of that sort they found the old lady, who had been sitting in back, lying across the lap of her daughter, who was in front, each soaked in her own and the other's blood indistinguishably, each so shattered and broken that there was no point whatever in an autopsy to determine whether it was broken neck or ruptured heart that caused death.

Overturning cars specialize in certain injuries. Cracked pelvis, for instance, guaranteeing agonizing months in bed, motionless, perhaps crippled for life—broken spine resulting from sheer sidewise twist—the minor details of smashed knees and splintered shoulder blades caused by crashing into the side of the car as she goes over with the swirl of an insane roller coaster—and the lethal consequences of broken ribs, which puncture hearts and lungs with their raw ends. The consequent internal hemorrhage is no less dangerous because it is the pleural instead of the abdominal cavity that is filling with blood.

Flying glass—safety glass is by no means universal yet—contributes much more than its share to the spectacular side of accidents. It doesn't merely cut—the fragments are driven in as if a cannon loaded with broken bottles had been fired in your face, and a sliver in the eye, traveling with such force, means certain blindness. A leg or arm stuck through the windshield will cut clean to the bone through vein, artery and muscle like a piece of beef under the butcher's knife, and it takes little time to lose a fatal amount of blood under such circumstances. Even safety glass may not be wholly safe when the car crashes something at high speed. You hear picturesque tales of how a flying human body will make a neat hole in the stuff with its head—the shoulders stick—the glass holds—and the raw, keen edge of the hole decapitates the body as neatly as a guillotine.

Or, to continue with the decapitation motif, going off the road into a post-and-rail fence can put you beyond worrying about other injuries immediately when a rail comes through the windshield and tears off your head with its splintery end—not as neat a job but thoroughly efficient. Bodies are often found with their shoes off and their feet all broken out of shape. The shoes are back on the floor of the car, empty and with their laces still neatly tied. That is the kind of impact produced by modern speeds.

But all that is routine in every American community. To be remembered individually by doctors and policemen, you have to do something as grotesque as the lady who burst the windshield with her head, splashing splinters all over the other occupants of the car, and then, as the car rolled over, rolled with it down the edge of the windshield frame and cut her throat from ear to ear. Or park on the pavement too near a curve at night and stand in front of the tail light as you take off the spare tire—which will immortalize you in somebody's memory as the fellow who was mashed three feet broad and two inches thick by the impact of a heavy duty truck against the rear of his own car. Or be as original as the pair of youths who were thrown out of an open roadster this spring —thrown clear—but each broke a windshield post with his head in passing and the whole top of each skull, down to the eyebrows, was missing. Or snap off a nine-inch tree and get yourself impaled by a ragged branch.

None of all that is scare-fiction; it is just the horrible raw material of the year's statistics as seen in the ordinary course of duty by policemen and doctors, picked at random. The surprising thing is that there is so little dissimilarity in the stories they tell.

It's hard to find a surviving accident victim who can bear to talk. After you come to, the gnawing, searing pain throughout your body is accounted for by learning that you have both collarbones smashed, both shoulder blades splintered, your right arm broken in three places and three ribs cracked, with every chance of bad internal ruptures. But the pain can't distract you, as the shock begins to wear off, from realizing that you are probably on your way out. You can't forget that, not even when they shift you from the ground to the stretcher and your broken ribs bite into your lungs and the sharp ends of your collarbones slide over to stab deep into each side of your screaming throat. When you've stopped screaming, it all comes back—you're dying and you hate yourself for it. That isn't fiction either. It's what it actually feels like to be one of that 36,000.

And every time you pass on a blind curve, every time you hit it up on a slippery road, every time you step on it harder than your reflexes will safely take, every time you drive with your reactions slowed down by a drink or two, every time you follow the man ahead too closely, you're gambling a few seconds against this kind of blood and agony and sudden death.

Take a look at yourself as the man in the white jacket shakes his head over you, tells the boys with the stretcher not to bother and turns away to somebody else who isn't quite dead yet. And then take it easy.

Lincoln Goes to Gettysburg

Condensed from Redbook Magazine

Carl Sandburg

Author of "Abraham Lincoln—The Prairie Years," and "The War Years," etc.

WHEN Governor Curtin of Pennsylvania set aside November 19, 1863, for the dedication of a National Soldiers' Cemetery at Gettysburg, the only invitation President Lincoln received to attend the ceremonies was a printed circular.

The duties of orator of the day had fallen on Edward Everett. An eminent figure, perhaps the foremost of all American classical orators, he had been Governor of Massachusetts, Ambassador to Great Britain and President of Harvard. There were four published volumes of his orations. His lecture on Washington, delivered 122 times in three years, had in 1859 brought a fund of $58,000, which he gave for the purchase of Mount Vernon as a permanent shrine.

Serene, suave, handsomely venerable in his 69th year, Everett was a natural choice of the Pennsylvania commissioners, who gave him two months to prepare his address. The decision to invite Lincoln to speak was an afterthought. As one of the commissioners later wrote: "The question was raised as to his ability to speak upon such a solemn occasion; the invitation was not settled upon until about two weeks before the exercises were held."

In these dark days Lincoln was far from popular in many quarters. Some newspapers claimed that the President was going to make a stump speech over the graves of the Gettysburg dead as a political show. Thaddeus Stevens, Republican floor leader in the House, believed in '63 that Lincoln was a "dead card" in the political deck. He favored Chase for the next President, and hearing that Lincoln and Secretary of State Seward were going to Gettysburg, he commented: "The dead going to bury the dead."

Copyright 1936, The McCall Co., 230 Park Ave., N. Y. C. (Redbook, June, '36)
Reprinted by permission of Harcourt, Brace & Co., Inc.

Selected from July 1936 issue of The Reader's Digest

On the day before the ceremony a special train decorated with red-white-and-blue bunting stood ready to take the presidential party to Gettysburg. When his escort remarked that they had no time to lose, Lincoln said he felt like an Illinois man who was going to be hanged, and as the man passed along the road on the way to the gallows, the crowds kept pushing into the way and blocking passage. The condemned man at last called out: "Boys, you needn't be in such a hurry; there won't be any fun till I get there."

Reaching Gettysburg, Lincoln was driven to a private residence on the public square. The sleepy little country town was overflowing. Private homes were filled with notables and nondescripts. Hundreds slept on the floors of hotels. Bands blared till late in the night. When serenaders called on the President for a speech, he responded: "In my position it is sometimes important that I should not say foolish things." (A voice: "If you can help it.") "It very often happens that the only way to help it is to say nothing at all. Believing that is my present condition this evening, I must beg of you to excuse me from addressing you further." The crowd didn't feel it was much of a speech. They went next door with the band and blared for Seward.

Beset with problems attendant on the conduct of the war, Lincoln had had little time to prepare his address. About ten o'clock that night before the ceremony he sat down in his room to do more work on it. It was midnight or later when he went to sleep.

At least 15,000 people were on Cemetery Hill for the exercises next day when the procession from Gettysburg arrived afoot and horseback. The President's horse seemed small for him. One of the commissioners, riding just behind the President, noted that he sat erect and looked majestic to begin with, and then got to thinking so his body leaned forward, his arms hung limp and his head bent far down.

The parade had begun to move at eleven, and in 15 minutes it was over. But the orator of the day had not arrived. Bands played till noon. Mr. Everett arrived. On the platform sat state governors, Army officers, foreign ministers, Members of Congress, the President and his party.

When Edward Everett was introduced, he bowed low to Lincoln, then stood in silence before a crowd that stretched to limits that would test his voice. Around were the wheat fields, the meadows, the peach orchards and beyond, the contemplative blue ridge of a low mountain range. He had taken note of these in his prepared and rehearsed address. "Overlooking these broad fields now reposing from the labors of the waning year, the mighty Alleghenies dimly towering before us, the graves of our brethren beneath our feet, it is with hesitation that I raise my poor voice to break the eloquent silence of God and Nature."

He proceeded: "It was appointed by law in Athens—" and gave an extended sketch of the manner in which the Greeks cared for their dead who fell in battle. He gave an outline of how the war began, traversed decisive features of the three days' battles at Gettysburg, denounced the doctrine of state sovereignty, drew parallels from European history, and came to his peroration quoting Pericles on dead patriots: "The whole earth is the sepulcher of illustrious men." He spoke for an hour and 57 minutes. It was the effort of his life, and embodied the perfections of the school of oratory in which he had spent his career.

When the time came for Lincoln to speak he put on his steel-bowed glasses, rose, and holding in one hand the two sheets of paper at which he occasionally glanced, he delivered the address in his high-pitched and clear-carrying voice. A photographer bustled about with his equipment, but before he had his head under the hood for an exposure, the President had said "by the people and for the people," and the nick of time was past for a photograph. The nine sentences were spoken in five minutes, and the applause was merely formal—a tribute to the occasion, to the high office, by persons who had sat as an audience for three hours.

That evening Lincoln took the train back to Washington. He was weary, talked little, stretched out on the seats and had a wet towel laid across his forehead. He felt that about all he had given the audience was ordinary garden-variety dedicatory remarks. "That speech," he said, "was a flat failure, and the people are disappointed."

Much of the newspaper reaction was more condemnatory. The *Patriot and Union* of nearby Harrisburg took its fling: "The President acted without sense and without constraint in a panorama that was gotten up more for the benefit of his party than for the honor of the dead. . . . We pass over the silly remarks of the President; for the credit of the nation we are willing that the veil of oblivion shall be dropped over them and that they shall no more be repeated or thought of." And the Chicago *Times* fumed: "The cheek of every American must tingle with shame as he reads the silly, flat and dish-watery utterances of the man who has to be pointed out to intelligent foreigners as the President of the United States." Wrote the correspondent of the London *Times,* "Anything more dull and commonplace it would not be easy to produce."

A reporter for the Chicago *Tribune,* however, telegraphed a prophetic sentence: "The dedicatory remarks of President Lincoln will live among the annals of man." The Philadelphia *Evening Bulletin* said thousands who would not read the elaborate oration of Mr. Everett would read the President's few words, "and not many will do it without a moistening of the eye and a swelling of the heart." And a writer in *Harper's Weekly:* "The oration by Mr. Everett was smooth and cold. . . . The few words of the President were from the heart to the heart. They cannot be read, even, without kindling emotion. 'The world will little note nor long remember what we say here, but it can never forget what they did here.' It was as simple and felicitous and earnest a word as was ever spoken."

Everett's opinion of the speech, written in a note to Lincoln the next day, was more than mere courtesy. "I should be glad if I could flatter myself that I came as near to the central idea of the occasion in two hours as you did in two minutes." Lincoln's immediate reply: "In our respective parts you could not have been excused to make a short address, nor I a long one. I am pleased to know that, in your judgment, the little I did say was not entirely a failure."

The Perfect Cook

The supreme cook of the world, when he arrives, will be one of French rearing who then went and learned about pastries in Vienna or Copenhagen, and about appetizers in Scandinavia and about soups in Russia and about sausages in Germany and about antipasti in Italy; and after that came over to this country to let a Down East housewife school him in pies and show him what moral grandeur abides in baked beans; and a Virginia or a Maryland woman teach him what can be done with crabs and oysters and terrapin; and an old-fashioned Louisiana lady introduce to him Creole gumbos and divers shrimp dishes; and a black mammy anywhere in the interior South instruct him in the right use of the frying pan; and a Mexican elucidate for him the delectable mysteries of commingled maize, red peppers and beans. As a finished product, he won't last long, though, in this lesser sphere. Blessed Providence will put forth its almighty hand and pluck him up to heaven to cook for the angels.   —Irvin S. Cobb in *Cosmopolitan*

The Case for Chastity

By

Margaret Culkin Banning

*In preparation for over a year, the following article was based on
extended research and interviews and on data supplied by doctors,
psychologists and others who deal daily with difficulties arising from
sex conduct. It may be said, therefore, to represent not only the author's own considered opinion, but also the best informed opinion of
the day. Mrs. Banning, mother of four children, is widely known for
her numerous articles on problems of youth, marriage and the family.*

IF THERE IS a case for chastity, it should be stated. Religion and
obedience to moral codes still settle the question for many. But
the increasing secularization of thought and the frequent denial
that any moral issue is involved in sex conduct leaves uncounted
thousands of young people today supposedly free to "make up their own
minds," if such a phrase can be used concerning conduct which is nearly
always the result of runaway emotion.

They make up their minds with insufficient knowledge and without
hearing the full argument. They are told that "everyone does it" and
that unchastity or even promiscuity "doesn't make any difference any
more." Thus misled, they may proceed to action which will almost
surely have a permanent effect on the life of any girl involved and which
in most cases alters her psychology as well as her physiology.

There are parked and lightless cars on side roads everywhere. There
is a "couple trade" at tourist cabins which cater to a few hours of
intimate occupancy. The dean of a coeducational university said to me
that almost every hotel in the city adjoining the campus was open to
boys who wanted to take girls to them for the night. From 1100 ques-
tionnaires sent to college students, 200 to post-college students, and from

Selected from August 1937 issue of The Reader's Digest

300 interviews, it seems plainly apparent that there remain few taboos about sex in the college groups, and that while some girls prefer to wait until marriage, they are not shocked by the sex experience of their friends. And we know that there are 50,000 unmarried mothers registered yearly in the United States; that through wealth and influence many unmarried mothers are not registered; that many couples marry after pregnancy is discovered; and that birth control and abortions prevent motherhood in most illicit affairs.

Nevertheless, we must remember that unchastity, common though it may be, is not the norm. That still is chastity. Society does not approve nor is it set up for the general practice of unchastity. Every adult must know, as I do, many young girls who are not troubled by this problem, and others whose lives offer no opportunity for it. They keep regular hours. They are preoccupied with study, sports, domestic tasks and wholesome social activities.

Yet they cannot but hear, and hence we adults cannot ignore, the widespread whispering campaign that is now condoning unchastity and even advocating premarital relations. So there is sound reason for going right after the facts and unveiling a few that may still be shrouded even in a period of frankness. Some parents believe that the subject should not be given publicity, lest argument increase undue curiosity or foster morbid interests. But it is secret rather than open discussion which creates morbidity; and, what is more, young people are increasingly frank among themselves, and adult silence only serves further to separate generations which are already quite far enough apart in matters of advice and sympathy.

Boys urging sex experience often say, "Why not?" and treat it as a matter of light concern. But it is revealing that no reputable physician who has handled thousands of cases and thousands of confidences is equally casual. No psychologist who has seriously investigated the problems of sexual relations outside of marriage treats them as trivial. That conscience and emotion will make the final decision in each case is obvious. But the personal and social consequences of unchastity, as they are apparent to those in a position to know, ought to be matters of public information.

First of all, there are the facts about venereal disease and abortion. The American Social Hygiene Association estimates that five percent of the American people have syphilis and ten percent have gonorrhea. The highest attack rate for syphilis occurs during the early adult years, 16 to 30. If venereal disease is ultimately stamped out, one risk of unchastity will be destroyed. But we are a long way from that yet. In the meantime, there is a serious and constant danger of disease in premarital relations because a girl does not go freely to her doctor for advice.

Some information comes her way—a great deal of it wrong. She is apt to believe she is safe from conception because of certain contraceptives. Here is a comment on that by Dr. Hannah Stone, Medical Director of Margaret Sanger's birth control clinic in New York:

> The best concerns offer absolutely unreliable contraceptives. A firm enjoying the respect of the medical profession advertises a vaginal jelly that is only about 60 percent safe. Suppositories on the market are between 40 and 50 percent safe. The strongest douche is successful about 10 percent of the time. The situation is further complicated by the fact that different women are susceptible to different contraceptives.

This is borne out by Dr. Maurice Bigelow, director of the Institute of Practical Science Research. His institute tested hundreds of rubber condoms bought from a reliable manufacturer and discarded 25 out of every 100 as being imperfect. The equipments involving chemicals lose their effectiveness unless perfectly fresh. In other words, "You're perfectly safe" is not only an ugly and abnormal statement but it happens to be untrue. The conditions commonly surrounding acts of unchastity make it doubly untrue.

Figures show beyond a doubt that a tremendous number of unmarried young women go to abortionists. No doubt many of them have heard the current claptrap about an abortion being nothing at all to endure. Let them also hear this: Ten thousand girls and women lose their lives each year at the hands of abortionists. Dr. Frederick J. Taussig says:

> The risk of infection is approximately ten times greater than at ordinary childbirth for the reason that the uterine cavity must be invaded, while in childbirth this is rarely the case. Also, for every woman who dies as a result of abortion, several women are disabled, sometimes permanently, or rendered sterile, or, at a subsequent pregnancy, suffer from the after effects of the abortion.

The medical point of view is not the only aspect to consider. The psychological effects of abortion are equally serious. Girls often suffer horror for the rest of their lives, as well as increasing grief for the lost child. An abortion may injure not only the woman's health but also her emotional outlook. In hours of childbirth a woman often resents

77

the results of her sex experience. But later she has the child to make up for the pain, and she has the protection of her husband and the respect of the community. The unmarried girl who goes to an abortionist has the resentment but neither the child nor a husband's protection to balance what may easily grow into hate of a man she loved, or perhaps dread of sex relations in a subsequent marriage.

These dangers—disease, abortion, emotional disasters, and even death —surround every premarital relation. But many people run the risks and escape. If the girl does escape, is there still no case for chastity? The argument for it certainly is not sound or effective if it rests only upon the fear of consequences.

Dr. Thomas Parran, Surgeon General of the United States, says, "I have always hoped that we could divest our social hygiene program from the fear motive. If gonorrhea and syphilis were unknown diseases, the ideal of monogamous sex relationship should, and I believe would, still stand upon its own intrinsic merits."

What, then, are these intrinsic values that make the case for chastity? Here is the conclusion of one young woman who went through an extra-marital experience:

> Much is talked of the evils of frustration in the case of the woman who denies herself the physical expression of love. In my opinion that vague and generally periodic torment is as nothing compared to the frustration suffered by the woman who seeks happiness in love outside of marriage. With all the latent instincts of her sex released and in-tensified by the mating experience, awake for the first time in her life to the full design of married love, she realizes with a sense of dumb defeat that for her the fulfillment of that design must remain, perhaps forever, an unaccomplished thing. It is a trapped, blind-alley feeling that only one who has experienced it can appreciate. The conflict set up as a result casts its dark shadow over an experience which one had expected to be all light and freedom.

There is far more to be said. Early and casual sex experience often inhibits and spoils mature experience. "Coming too soon," writes L. S. Hollingsworth in his *Psychology of the Adolescent*, "it may block maturity by putting the emphasis on physical release"—as against the mature satisfaction which includes mental and esthetic elements. There are plenty of girls who pride themselves on never "going any farther than petting" without any idea of how disastrously far they have already gone. The dean of a woman's college, after considerable research, states that petting is apt to create habits which give a semblance of satisfaction without intercourse and so unsuit a girl emotionally for marriage. One authority has declared flatly that petting is far more dangerous than the complete sex act, for it can ruin normal sex experience. Following many consultations, a psychologist of the Y.W.C.A. says that substitute satisfactions tend to make intercourse an anti-climax. Over-stimulated and wrongly stimulated, girls who have indulged in petting find it difficult to respond to normal sex relations, and their chances of satisfaction and compatibility in marriage are very poor indeed.

The question of where to stop is not easy to answer. But any girl can differentiate between the romantic embrace which is a natural expression of young love and experiments in sexual sensation. She can differentiate, that is, as long as she is reacting normally, and here one cannot possibly ignore the influence of drinking. Alcohol inflames the senses, is an acknowledged aphrodisiac in most cases. A girl who has been drinking, and especially the girl who is not used to drinking, cannot possibly stand guard over her judgment or her conduct. And even if she keeps command of herself and "knows what she is doing," I doubt if she knows that doctors and psychologists think that by petting she may be doing herself a possibly permanent injury.

And if the girl goes, as they say, "all the way," what does she confront? Each girl's chastity is the interweaving of her moral code, her nervous system, her physical being, and her mind. Does she realize how profoundly that interwoven fabric may be altered in a few yielding moments?

In the breaking down of chastity, her moral code is often violated. True, she may think she has none. Yet the great weight of tradition and poetry and romance is pressing on her, even if she is without a belief in orthodox religion. Hence many girls cannot but carry with them into early sexual experience a sense of sin which they never lose. This "guilt sense" is spoken of by almost all the doctors who have investigated such things. Even without a sense of actual sin against religion, the "guilt sense" persists in a large majority of cases.

The girl who thus feels that she is doing wrong suffers shockingly. The wound in her conscience may heal and harden and make her into a liar, or it may never heal so that she will go about with an actual fear of punishment and retribution. Often she confuses her sexual disappointments with the punishment due to sin.

On the other hand, there are girls who have really cast off conventions—who feel no spiritual or moral connection with their sex conduct. How do they come out? Usually they are deserted. If a woman has this point of view, she almost always believes—and says so once too often—that she can look out for herself. In many cases that is what her lover ultimately allows her to do. And then she becomes an outlaw. Society provides no protection for her. She may have the bravado of the outlaw, but she also has his loneliness.

One authority points out that there is growing up a large body of women who, because they were deserted by their first lover, or have found emotional release without the responsibility of marriage, are remaining unmarried and childless. This group is not only dangerous to other marriages but tragic in itself. Many are intellectual, healthy people who should be reproducing themselves instead of leading one-sided, uncreative lives.

So though people may say that morality is no longer involved in this question, I think they talk nonsense. Unchastity does affect the moral system, if only to set a girl's hand against society. Many girls fancy themselves in that rôle, rebels against a social system they consider stuffy, and religions they consider obsolete. But these girls do not know what they combat, what protections they will strip from their future life, and what a weight of experience and history is against them.

The effect of unchastity on the nervous system is as serious. Being clandestine, it is rarely either well housed or comfortable. It lodges but does not live. Think of the wayside cabins, the cheap hotels, the back seats of cars, as an environment for what we call love. Hurried, watchful, fearful of interruption or discovery—these are inevitable descriptions of unchastity.

On this point it is hard to find any more competent conclusions than those of Dr. Oliver M. Butterfield, director of the Family Guidance Service in New York:

> The sexual adjustment is not a simple thing to make under the best of conditions and when hampered by guilt and apprehension it is almost impossible. At a time when man and woman may need expert advice they are forced to hide their relationship. Because of this secrecy many things are likely to happen. If the woman is a virgin she may need medical attention before she can have intercourse. The sex act is not instinctive. Premarital relationships can build up, through ignorance, incorrect, unsatisfying behavior that must be painfully unlearned after marriage.

The ordinary situation of unchastity is the case, then, of an apprehensive pair of people, in an uncongenial or uncomfortable environment, wondering if anyone has seen them. What harm such experiences do to the nervous systems of young girls, who are at such times under the added strain of great excitement, cannot be measured.

It is generally agreed that repressions are bad for almost everyone, and that argument is often given for indulgence in unchastity. But it works the other way too. Loudly as it may boast of its freedom, unchastity carries repression right along with it. There are places where it cannot go. The unchaste girl often lacks escort and open companionship. There are times when she may not speak to the one person she cares about. As long as passionate love or even excitement is growing and deeply shared, this may not matter. Secrecy is then a delicious privacy. But every recorded experience shows that such secrecy has the seeds of bitterness in it. The girl usually becomes resentful, hating to be hidden and unacknowledged, and yet more fearful of the discovery of her relation.

Of course, the couple may marry. But they still are cheating themselves. They enter on the responsibilities and adjustments of living together, take up the hard work that marriage is, without the delights and fresh discoveries which make those responsibilities pleasurable and easy. Even with its natural rewards and emotional impetus, marriage is difficult enough. But if the end of romance has already been reached before a couple marry, they face its problems without the natural compensation for them. They are apt to be jealous, for each knows the other as an experimenter.

On the other hand, the relationship is more than likely to be broken off. Remember, it is with the immature that we are chiefly concerned—the young people who are thinking only of an immediate pleasure, an adventure. They have heard that youthful sex experiments may be casual, carefree and harmless. But have the girls who act on this heard also what the best medical and psychological authority has to say—that a first sex adventure can rarely be either casual or carefree to any normal girl? That it will not satisfy the mating instinct, but will only arouse it more powerfully, and fix it upon one individual? Most girls feel that there is a tie-up between sexual and spiritual experience, and associate sexual experience closely with the identity of the lover. But if the adventure is, as it very well may be, casual in fact to the boy in the case, who passes on to other conquests, the consequences to the girl can only be torments of jealousy, frustration and despair.

Such breaks and the resultant sense of inferiority and pain often make a woman promiscuous. Not a voice of the slighest authority is raised for promiscuity. Doctors may and do differ in their vehemence as to what harm the premarital relation does, but as far as the harm of promiscuity is concerned, for either a woman or a man, they are completely agreed.

The promiscuous woman is usually in doubt of her own attractiveness and is seeking reassurance by repeated and varied experience with men. The fact of inferiority is also true of promiscuous men, who in such ways prove a virility which they secretly doubt. It is bad for a man who ultimately wants a happy home relation because he soon becomes neither romantic nor patient enough to give his wife satisfaction. Also, the promiscuous man or woman finds adjustment to monogamy almost impossible. An unchaste past is intrusive and a trouble maker. Sex loses charm, but the craving for satisfaction and the nervous search for it goes on. Promiscuity makes people lose the greatest experience in life—love.

It is all very well to say, "People look at these things differently today." They may look at them differently, but they feel about the same.

Jealousy, for example, is still very much alive. It is true that reason is having a quieting effect among well-bred people. But, on the other hand, it is reason itself which often argues with a man that if his wife was unchaste before marriage, she has already destroyed certain inhibitions, which makes her more apt to be unfaithful. Psychologists say, too, that the promiscuous woman often suffers the most of all from jealousy.

Again, we cannot ignore man's preference for a virgin as wife. As to this we have the testimony of those who have built up records from cases. The preference is both modern and historic truth. Westermarck's *History of Marriage* bears testimony to that. Though boys of today may talk big and pretend to indifference, they still don't want the girl they love to have had previous possessors. So it is as true now as ever that in sacrificing chastity a girl may be gambling away her later chances of lifelong married happiness.

As a matter of fact, we have not so much that is new to add to what history teaches about sex. It is incorrect to say that we are reverting to savagery when sex conduct becomes lax. Among savage tribes, sex behavior was always subject to rules, though they were not like our own. What history very clearly reveals is that there have always been laws governing chastity. These are often the oldest primary laws, and infringement of them was subject to grave punishment because it presented complications of life and excited angers and conflicts which were bitter.

Unless sexual relations are to become disintegrating, there is always a necessity of trust between the individuals concerned. Such trust is usually not sustained after the first height of passion has been reached and passed, unless it is connected with the religion or the philosophy of man or woman—whatever ties the person up to life itself. It is not sentimental but hard fact that sex relationship either has to be connected with a moral code which is self-sustaining (and this is very rare indeed), or it has to be based on a belief that sexual relations involve a duty to the race as well as to the individual Olga Knopf puts the case plainly when she says that "sexual relations are not private affairs alone. They are the concern of the whole of society."

That is what young people, those who are still only curious and those who are already on the defensive, should be helped to understand. Without scolding, or without minimizing the rights of individual love, it ought to be shown that though the laws involving marriage may be evaded and broken, they do exist and penalties are still exacted for their infraction.

Now if you could make the young couple in the back of the car or in the tourist cabin believe this in advance, nothing would be better. But how? The boy and girl are young, eager, and together. They have to be shown first of all that those who wish to control the mating instinct are by no means plotting against their attraction for each other, but against the influences that will do violence to their love—or what might in the end become love.

The thing to do is to help these young couples out, and, if their attraction is not casual, to encourage their marriage. As the authorities who were interviewed on this subject of chastity made their comments, the statement came again and again with repeated emphasis that the best solution was early marriage. This is not by any means synonymous with hasty marriage. But if a boy and a girl felt that they did not have to face an indefinite postponement of sex relations, their attitude would change. It is the hopelessness cast in their faces, the long gap between the awakening of their passion and its decently authorized expression which makes for rebellion against conventions and accepted rules.

We hear on all sides that economic conditions make early marriage difficult now. But it has never been very easy for young people to marry. Throughout history we see that parents have always had to help them out at the start. And modern parents, say those who know best, should be ready to do likewise; should encourage early marriage. But they should also frankly state the case for premarital chastity.

For there is, as we have seen, such a case. Men have devised no way of protecting the unchaste woman, except in some cases from childbearing and disease. She is in danger of moral and psychological breakdown. Unchastity gives the richest experience in life the poorest and most ignoble surroundings. It checks and stunts the development of love. It breeds lonely women and selfish men.

Finally, normal young men and women do not want unchastity. They are searching for an ethic to guide them. College investigations show that students believe in fidelity, want marriage. They want an emotional life with vitality in it, one that will wear. The case for chastity does not need much pleading before young people thus disposed. Given proper ideals, decent upbringing, half a chance, it is what girls and boys want.

Experts, doctors, psychologists and friends may advise. But they do not decide in the end. This is one of the social problems which is broken up into individual cases for decision. Out of this tangle of impulses, some of them inherited and some the product of immediate environment, the burden of the race as well as individual happiness is laid upon each boy and girl. The attitude toward chastity is as important a matter as may come to each one of them in a whole lifetime. That means that the effort of their elders should be to keep plainly before them all these scientific, spiritual and historical arguments for chastity which will strengthen their own normal resistance to the laxness they are aware of around them.

The Astor Test

At a large banquet Lady Astor once remarked that men were vainer than women and, meeting with stormy opposition, declared herself ready to substantiate her statement. Steering the conversation to men's fashions, she suddenly said in a loud voice:

"It's a pity that the most intelligent and learned men attach least importance to the way they dress. Why, right at this table the most cultivated man is wearing the most clumsily knotted tie!"

As if on a given signal, every man in the room immediately put his hand to his tie to straighten it. —*L'Humeur* (Paris)

Mother of Comptons

Condensed from The Scientific Monthly

Milton S. Mayer

ONORARY DEGREES are supposed to signify achievement—sometimes achievement in science or the arts, sometimes (though
seldom openly) the achievement of the college in wheedling a
new dormitory from a prosperous citizen. A few years ago Ohio's
historic Western College for Women bestowed a doctorate of laws for
neither of these reasons. To a woman, youthful at 74, it awarded the
LL.D. "for outstanding achievement as wife and mother of Comptons."
    The ceremony over, the new doctor hurried back to the welcome ob-
scurity of an old frame house in Wooster, Ohio. Otelia Compton doesn't
want to be famous, and she isn't. But her four children are.
    Those who extol the virtues of heredity may examine with profit the
Compton family tree. The ancestors of the first family of science were
farmers and mechanics. The only one of them associated with scholar-
ship was a carpenter who helped nail together the early buildings of
Princeton. There was no reason to predict that the union of Elias
Compton and Otelia Augspurger, two country schoolteachers, would
produce columns in *Who's Who*.
    Yet Karl, their oldest son, is a distinguished physicist, now president
of the great scientific institution, Massachusetts Institute of Technology;
Mary, the second child, is principal of a missionary school in India and
wife of the president of Allahabad Christian College; Wilson, the
third, is a noted economist and lawyer, and is general manager of the
Lumber Manufacturers' Association; while Arthur, the "baby," is, at 45,
one of the immortals of science—winner of the Nobel Prize in Physics.
    How did it happen? The answer, according to the four famous
Comptons, is contained in the old frame house in Wooster. Elias
Compton was the beloved elder statesman of Ohio education; he taught
philosophy at Wooster College for 45 years. But he always explained that
he was just one of Otelia's boys. All credit was hers.

Copyright 1938, The Science Press, Grand Central Terminal, N. Y. C.
(The Scientific Monthly, November, '38)

Selected from November 1938 issue of The Reader's Digest

85

Otelia Compton, characteristically, denies that she has a recipe for rearing great men and women. She will admit that her children are "worthy," but what the world calls great has small significance for her. When Arthur won the world's highest award in science, her first words were, "I hope it doesn't turn his head." The only way I was able to pry her loose from her reticence was to get her into a good hot argument.

There is nothing unfair about picking an intellectual quarrel with this woman of 79; she is more than equal to it. She reads as ardently as any scholar. She thinks as nimbly as any logician. One day this summer, her children kidded her about getting old. It seems she forgot to take off her wrist watch before her daily swim.

Cornered in her kitchen, Otelia Compton simply had to admit that she knows something about motherhood. There are her four children, with their total of 31 college and university degrees and their memberships in 39 learned societies. In addition, there are the hundreds of boys and girls whose lives Otelia Compton shaped during the 35 years she spent directing the Presbyterian Church's two homes for the children of its missionaries.

Her formula is so old it is new, so orthodox it is radical, so commonplace that we have forgotten it and it startles us. "We used the Bible and common sense," she told me.

Did she think heredity important?

That was easy for the descendant of Alsatian farmers. "If you mean the theory that worth is handed down in a blue bloodstream, I don't think much of it. Lincoln's 'heredity' was nil. Dissolute kings and worthless descendants of our 'best families' are pretty sad evidence. No, I've seen too many extraordinary men and women who were children of the common people to put much stock in that.

"But there is a kind of heredity that is all-important. That is the heredity of training. A child isn't likely to learn good habits from his parents unless they learned them from their parents. Call that environment if you want to, or environmental heredity. But it is something that is handed down from generation to generation."

She feels strongly that too many Americans today are obsessed with the notion that their children "haven't got a chance." "This denial of the reality of opportunity," she said, "suggests a return to the medieval psychology of a permanently degraded peasant class. Once parents decide their children haven't got a chance, they are not likely to give them one. And the children, in turn, become imbued with this paralyzing attitude of futility."

Certainly the four young Comptons would never have had a chance had their parents regarded limited means as insuperable. Elias Compton was earning $1400 a year while his wife was rearing four children and maintaining the kind of home a college community demands. The children all had their chores, but household duties—and here is an ingredient of the Compton recipe—were never allowed to interfere either with school work or the recreation that develops healthy bodies and sportsmanship.

If heredity is not the answer, I wanted to know, what is?

"The home."

"That's a pleasant platitude," I said.

"It's a forgotten platitude," she replied sharply. "The tragedy of American life is that the home is becoming incidental at a time when it is needed as never before. Parents forget that neither school nor the world can reform the finished product of a bad home. They forget that their children are their first responsibility.

"The first thing parents must remember is that their children are not likely to be any better than they are themselves. Mothers and fathers who wrangle and dissipate need not be surprised if their observant young ones take after them. The next thing is that parents must obtain the confidence of their children in all things if they do not want to make strangers of them and have them go to the boy on the street corner for advice. Number three is that parents must explain to the child every action that affects him, even at the early age when parents believe, usually mistakenly, that the child is incapable of understanding. Only thus will the child mature with the sense that justice has been done him and develop the impulse to be just himself.

"The mother or father who laughs at a youngster's 'foolish' ideas forgets that those ideas are not foolish to the child. When Arthur was 10 years old he wrote an essay taking issue with experts on why some elephants were three-toed and others five-toed. He brought it to me to read, and I had a hard time keeping from laughing. But I knew how seriously he took his ideas, so I sat down and worked on them with him."

Arthur—he of the Nobel Prize—was listening. "If you had laughed at me that day," he interrupted, "I think you would have killed my interest in research."

"The reason why many parents laugh at their children," Mrs. Compton went on, "is that they have no interest in the child's affairs. It isn't enough to encourage the child; the parents must *participate* in

87

his interests. They must work *with* him, and if his interest turns out to be something about which they know nothing it is their business to educate themselves. If they don't the child will discover their ignorance and lose his respect for them."

When Karl Compton was 12, he wrote a "book" on Indian fighting. Mary was absorbed with linguistics. Wilson's devotion to the spitball made him the greatest college pitcher in the Middle West. Arthur, too, was a notable athlete, but his first love was astronomy. The combination of Indian fighting, linguistics, the spitball, and astronomy might have driven a lesser woman to despair, but Otelia Compton mastered them all.

When the four children were still under 10 years of age their mother took them to the wilds of northern Michigan where they hewed a clearing and pitched a tent. There these urban-bred children learned simplicity and hard work. There they imbibed, as the mother of Comptons would have every town child imbibe, of the unity and mystery of Nature.

The boys all worked summers and in college, gaining priceless experience; and they all had their own bank accounts, "not," their mother explains, "because we wanted them to glorify money but because we wanted them to learn that money, however much or however little, should never be wasted."

Would she put hard work first in her lexicon? Mrs. Compton thought a moment. "Yes," she said, "I would. That is, hard work in the right direction. The child who has acquired such habits does not need anything else."

And what is the "right kind" of hard work?

"The kind of work that is good in itself."

"What's wrong with working for money?" I asked.

The mother of Comptons exploded. "Everything! To teach a child that money-making for the sake of money is worthy is to teach him that the only thing worth while is what the world calls success. That kind of success has nothing to do either with usefulness or happiness. Parents teach it and the schools teach it, and the result is an age that thinks that money means happiness. The man who lives for money never gets enough, and he thinks that that is why he isn't happy. The real reason is that he has had the wrong goal of life set before him."

What did she mean by parents and schools "teaching" that money is happiness?

"I mean all this talk about 'careers' and 'practical' training. Children

88

should be taught how to think, and thinking isn't always practical. Children should be encouraged to develop their natural bents and not forced to choose a 'career.' When our children were still in high school, a friend asked Elias what they were going to be. His answer was, "I haven't asked them." Some of our neighbors thought we were silly when we bought Arthur a telescope and let him sit up all night studying the stars. It wasn't 'practical'."

Yet it was his "impractical" love of the stars that brought him the Nobel Prize and something over $20,000; and in order that he might pursue his cosmic ray research, the University of Chicago equipped a $100,000 laboratory for him.

I thought of the four Comptons and I wondered if "impractical" parents weren't perhaps the most practical.

I Got a Glory

On a day memorable to me, I boarded a tiny tugboat that I used often in crossing a southern river and saw that we had a new Negro engineer. He sat in the doorway of the engine room reading the Bible; he was fat, squat and black, but immaculate, and in his eyes was the splendor of ancient wisdom and peace with the world. As I paused to talk with him I noticed that the characteristic odors that had always emanated from the engine room were no longer there. And the engine! It gleamed and shone; from beneath its seat all the bilge-water was gone. Instead of grime and filth and stench I found beauty and order. When I asked the engineer how in the world he had managed to clean up the old room and the old engine, he answered in words that would go far toward solving life's main problems for many people.

"Cap'n," he said, nodding fondly in the direction of the engine, "it's just this way: I got a glory."

Making that engine the best on the river was his glory in life, and having a glory he had everything. The only sure way out of suffering that I know is to find a glory, and to give to it the strength we might otherwise spend in despair.

—Archibald Rutledge, *It Will Be Daybreak Soon* (Revell)

"In our seven years of publication," said the editors of *Story*, "no story has created so much excited comment as *Address Unknown*. The entire issue containing it was sold out within ten days."

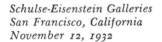

ADDRESS UNKNOWN

Condensed from Story

Kressmann Taylor

Schulse-Eisenstein Galleries
San Francisco, California
November 12, 1932

Herrn Martin Schulse
Schloss Rantzenburg
Munich, Germany

MY DEAR MARTIN:

Back in Germany! How I envy you! Although I have not seen it since my school days, the spell of *Unter den Linden* is still strong upon me—the discussions, the music, the lighthearted comradeship. And now the old Junker spirit, the Prussian arrogance and militarism are gone. You go to a democratic Germany.

Of course you are right to go. You never became American despite your success here, and now that the business is so well established you and Elsa must take your boys back to the homeland to be educated.

The business continues to go well. Mrs. Levine has bought the small Picasso at our price, for which I congratulate myself, and I have old Mrs. Fleshman playing with the notion of buying that hideous Madonna.

A delightful letter came yesterday from Griselle. She writes that she is about to make me proud of my little sister. She has the lead in a new play in Vienna and the notices are excellent. Poor child, it has not been easy for her, but she has never complained. She asked about you, Martin, in a very friendly way. Bitterness passes quickly when one

Copyright 1938, Story Magazine, Inc., 432 Fourth Ave., N. Y. C.
(Story, September–October, '38)

Selected from January 1939 issue of The Reader's Digest

is as young as she is. Of course neither of you was to be blamed. Those things are like quick storms, for a moment you are drenched and blasted, then it passes, and although you have neither quite forgotten, there remains only gentleness and no sorrow.

I have not yet written her that you are in Europe but I know she would be glad to feel that friends are not far away.

With the most affectionate remembrances to Elsa and the boys,

MAX

●

Schloss Rantzenburg
Munich, Germany
December 10, 1932

Mr. Max Eisenstein
Schulse-Eisenstein Galleries
San Francisco, California

MAX, DEAR OLD FELLOW:

The check and accounts came through promptly, for which my thanks. Here at Munich we are established, but what a turmoil! The house I got at an amazing bargain. Thirty rooms and about ten acres of park, you would never believe it. But then, you could not appreciate how poor is now this sad land of mine. To Elsa's family we seem millionaires, for our American income places us among the wealthy here. The better foods are high in price and there is much political unrest even now under the presidency of Hindenburg, a fine liberal whom I much admire.

You write of Griselle. So she wins her success, the lovely one! I rejoice with you, although even now I resent it that she must struggle to win her way alone. Although you were silent during our stormy affair, you know that our decision was not easy. For Griselle I keep a tenderness that will last long after she has married someone else.

You must urge her to make contact with us. Elsa will welcome your sister, as she would welcome you. Give her our most warm congratulations for her success.

MARTIN

●

San Francisco
January 21, 1933

MY DEAR MARTIN:

I was glad to forward your address to Griselle. What jollification there will be when she sees you all! And I too shall be with you in spirit.

91

The oils you sent for the gallery are excellent, and the prices amazing. I shall dispose of them at an appalling profit almost at once. And the ugly Madonna is gone! Yes, to old Mrs. Fleshman. How I exulted as she bore the horror off, you alone will know.

Who is this Adolf Hitler who seems rising toward power in Germany? I do not like what I read of him.

Your ever affectionate

MAX

●

Munich
March 25, 1933

DEAR OLD MAX:

You have heard of course of the new events in Germany. I tell you truly, Max, I think in many ways Hitler is good for Germany, but I am not sure. The man is like an electric shock, strong as only a great orator and a zealot can be. But I ask myself, is he quite sane? His brown-shirt troops are of the rabble. They pillage and have started a bad Jew-baiting. But these may be minor things, the little surface scum when a big movement boils up. For I tell you, my friend, there is a surge—a surge. The people everywhere have had a quickening. The old despair has been thrown aside like a forgotten coat. A leader is found! Yet cautiously to myself I ask, a leader to where?

Publicly, as is natural, I express no doubt. I am now an official and a worker in the new regime and I exult very loud indeed.

So much for politics. Ourselves, we delight in our new home and have done much entertaining. Tonight the mayor is our guest, at a dinner for 28. We spread ourselves a little, maybe, but that is to be forgiven.

Meanwhile, our hearts go out to you across the wide sea, and when the glasses are filled we toast "Uncle Max."

Yours in affectionate regard,

MARTIN

●

Eisenstein Galleries
San Francisco
May 18, 1933

DEAR MARTIN:

I am in distress at the reports that come pouring in to us from the Fatherland, picturing a terrible pogrom, and I turn to you for light. I know that from you I can have the truth. These things may be, as you have said, but the brutal surface froth of revolution. But to us Jews it is almost unbelievable that the old familiar martyrdom must be endured in a civilized nation today. Write me, my friend, and set my mind at ease.

Griselle's play will close in June after a great success. She has a very fine offer in Berlin for the autumn, but I have written her to wait until the anti-Jewish feeling has abated.

Forgive me for so distrait a letter but I cannot rest until you have reassured me.

MAX

●

Deutsch-Voelkische Bank und
Handelsgesellschaft, München
July 9, 1933

DEAR MAX:

You see that I write upon the stationery of my bank. This is necessary because I have a request to make and I wish to avoid the new censorship which is most strict. We must for the present discontinue writing. If a communication becomes necessary you must enclose it with the bank draft and not write to me at my house.

As for the stern measures that so distress you, I myself did not like them at first, but I have come to see their painful necessity. The Jewish race is a sore spot to any nation that harbors it. I have never hated the individual Jew—yourself I have always cherished as a friend, but in all honesty I have loved you, not because of your race but in spite of it.

But this Jew trouble is only an incident. Something bigger is happening. If I could show you, if I could make you see—the rebirth of this new Germany under our Gentle Leader! In defeat for 14 years we bowed our heads in shame and poverty. But now we are free men. We purge our bloodstream of its baser elements, rise in our might and hold our heads up before the nations.

But no. I am sure you will not see how necessary is all this for Germany. You will not see that a few must suffer for the millions to be saved. You will be a Jew first and wail for your people. This is the Semitic character. You lament but you are never brave enough to fight back. That is why there are pogroms.

I regret our correspondence must close this way, Max.

Perhaps we can someday meet again on a field of better understanding.

As ever your

MARTIN SCHULSE

93

San Francisco
September 5, 1933

DEAR MARTIN:

Enclosed are your draft and the month's accounts. It is of necessity that I send a brief message. Griselle has gone to Berlin. She is too daring. But she has waited so long for success, and she laughs at my fears. She will be at the König Theater.

You are an official. For old friendship's sake, I beg of you watch over her. Go to Berlin if you can and see whether she is in danger.

Your new attitude I cannot discuss. But understand me. I did not expect you would take up arms for my people because they are my people, but because you were a man who loved justice.

I commend my rash Griselle to you. The child does not realize what a risk she is taking. I shall not write again.

Good-bye, my friend.

MAX

●

San Francisco
November 5, 1933

MARTIN:

I write again because I must. A black foreboding possesses me. I wrote Griselle in Berlin and she answered briefly. Rehearsals were going brilliantly; the play would open shortly. My second letter has been returned to me, marked only *Adressat Unbekannt.* Addressee unknown—what a darkness those words carry! How can she be unknown? It is surely a message that she has come to harm. They know what has happened to her, those stamped letters say, but I am not to know. This they tell me in two words, *Adressat Unbekannt.*

Martin, need I ask you to find her? Do not attempt to write to me. I know I need not even ask you to aid. It is enough to tell you that she must be in danger.

I leave her in your hands, for I am helpless.

MAX

●

San Francisco
November 23, 1933

MARTIN:

I turn to you in despair. For two months there has been only silence from Griselle, and now dread rumors begin to come. She appeared in

94

the Berlin play for a week. Then she was jeered from the audience as a Jewess. She is so headstrong, she threw the word back in their teeth. She told them proudly that she *was* a Jewess.

Some of the audience started after her, but she escaped and took refuge with a Jewish family. After several days, she changed her appearance as much as she could and started south, hoping to walk back to Vienna. She did not dare try the railroads. She told those she left that she would be safe if she could reach friends in Munich. That is my hope, that she has gone to you, for she has never reached Vienna. God grant you can send me a word of relief!   MAX

●

*Deutsch-Voelkische Bank und
Handelsgesellschaft, München
December 8, 1933*

DEAR MAX:

Heil Hitler! I much regret that I have bad news for you. Your sister is dead.

Unfortunately she was, as you have said, very much a fool. Not quite a week ago she came here, with a bunch of storm troopers almost right behind her. By luck I answer the door. At first I think it is an old woman and then I see the face, and then I see the storm troopers have turned in the park gates. Can I hide her? It is one chance in thousands.

Can I risk being arrested for harboring a Jew and lose all I have built up here?

"You will destroy us all, Griselle," I tell her. "You must run back further in the park." She looks at me and smiles (she was always a brave girl) and makes her own choice.

"I would not bring you harm, Martin," she says, and she runs toward the trees. But she must be tired. She does not run very fast and the storm troopers catch her. I am helpless. I go in the house and in a few minutes she stops screaming, and in the morning I have the body sent away for burial. She was a fool to come to Germany. Poor little Griselle.

I grieve with you, but as you see, I was helpless to aid her.

I must now demand you do not write again. I cannot tell how soon they may start to open the mail to the bank. It is not so good for me that a Jewess came here for refuge, and no further association can be tolerated.

A new Germany is being shaped here. We will soon show the world great things under our Glorious Leader.   MARTIN

ADDRESS UNKNOWN

Cablegram

MARTIN SCHULSE
MUNICH JANUARY 2, 1934

> YOUR TERMS ACCEPTED PAN EXHIBITION MAY FIRST PREPARE LEAVE FOR MOSCOW IF MARKET OPENS UNEXPECTEDLY FINANCIAL INSTRUCTIONS MAILED YOUR NEW ADDRESS

EISENSTEIN

●

San Francisco
January 3, 1934

Herrn Martin Schulse
Schloss Rantzenburg
Munich, Germany

OUR DEAR MARTIN:

Don't forget grandma's birthday. She will be 64 on the 8th. American contributors will furnish 1000 brushes for your German Young Painters' League. Mandelberg has joined in supporting the League. You must send 11 Picasso reproductions, 20 by 90, to branch galleries on the 25th, no sooner. Reds and blues must predominate. We can allow you $8000 on this transaction.

Our prayers follow you daily, dear brother.

EISENSTEIN

●

San Francisco
January 17, 1934

MARTIN, DEAR BROTHER:

Good news! The Fleishmans have advanced another $10,000. This will fill your Young Painters' League quota for a month but let us know if opportunities increase. Swiss miniatures are having a vogue. You must watch the market and plan to be in Zurich after May first.

Uncle Solomon will be very glad to see you and I know that you can rely heavily on his judgment.

Our hopes will follow your new efforts.

Success to you!

EISENSTEIN

●

Munich
February 12, 1934

MAX, MY OLD FRIEND:

My God, Max, do you know what you do? I shall try to smuggle this letter out with an American. I write in appeal from a despair you cannot imagine. This crazy cable! These letters you have sent. I am called in to account for them and they demand I give them the code. A code? How can you, a friend of long years, do this to me?

Already the results of your madness are terrible. I am bluntly told I must resign my office.

Yes, yes, I know why you do it—but do you not understand I could do nothing? What could I have done? I did not dare to try. I beg of you, not for myself, but for Elsa and the boys—think what it means to them if I am taken away and they do not know if I live or die.

Do you know what it is to be taken to a concentration camp? I beg of you, stop. I am in fear for my life—for my life, Max!

I have loved you like a brother, my old Maxel. My God, have you no mercy? I beg you, Max, no more, no more! Stop while I can be saved. From a heart filled with old affection I ask it.

MARTIN

●

San Francisco
March 3, 1934

OUR DEAR MARTIN:

A shipment of 1500 brushes should reach the Berlin branch for your painters by this week-end. This will allow time for practice before the big exhibition. American patrons will help with all the supplies.

Young Blum left last Friday with the Picasso specifications. He will leave oils in Hamburg and Leipzig and will then place himself at your disposal. We leave all final plans to your discretion but urge an early date for wholly successful exhibit.

The God of Moses be at your right hand.

EISENSTEIN

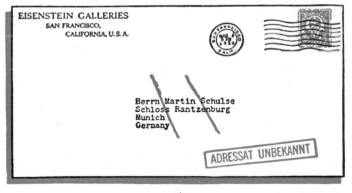

EISENSTEIN GALLERIES
SAN FRANCISCO,
CALIFORNIA, U. S. A.

Herrn Martin Schulse
Schloss Rantzenburg
Munich
Germany

ADRESSAT UNBEKANNT

FAMINE FIGHTERS
By Paul de Kruif

By training, PAUL DE KRUIF is himself a microbe hunter. After seven years as a bacteriologist, first at the University of Michigan, then at the Rockefeller Institute in New York, he found that the pen could be mightier than the test tube. In such books as MICROBE HUNTERS, MEN AGAINST DEATH, WHY KEEP THEM ALIVE?, THE FIGHT FOR LIFE, he has described to an ever wider public the drama, the trials and triumphs of science's struggle for a healthier mankind.

INTO Hillman Hospital in Birmingham, Alabama, certain sick people are brought on stretchers. They are stuporous, demented—yes, sometimes dying—from chronic famine. Ten years ago they would have had a 50.50 chance of not coming out alive. Today our famine fighters work what they dare to call, in cold scientific print, a miracle. Now a few cents' worth of chemical often sends such folks walking home the day they come into the hospital on a stretcher.

It is next door to resurrection.

Here is the beginning of a revolution in medical science. Here is yesterday's vague promise of vitamins, transformed by chemists into life-saving and life-giving power that's as magical as it is unexpected. Out of cheap coal tar these supercooks have refined to crystal purity the B vitamins hidden in the bones gnawed by cave men, the soups and stews of slaves and peasants, the salads and roasts of kings.

This is the testimony of my own eyes: women brought into the Nutrition Clinic of Hillman Hospital, forgetful, weak, crying uncontrollably, unable to care for their families. Some doctors would have wagged their heads, mumbling "neurasthenia" or "psychoneurosis." I saw how doses of new pure chemicals changed such women from sad to cheerful, hopeful human beings, in a few hours.

Their "nervous breakdowns" were only chemical.

So today at Hillman Hospital hundreds of people are given life and strength they never felt before. They come suffering from that old curse of Southern poverty, pellagra, in one or many of its myriad forms. But here's what's been discovered at Hillman Hospital: this is no single sickness. It is a complex of hidden starvations for certain chemicals, now definitely known. Here's what's new: this chronic chemical famine masquerades under many long-named medical illnesses

Selected from December 1940 issue of The Reader's Digest

—insanities, skin diseases, intestinal ailments, nervous breakdowns.

And it is by no means confined to Southern have-nots. It is nation-wide. It's rampant among millions of the middle class who believe their diets to be ample. It's now diagnosed among debutantes, even among doctors who thought their nutrition was balanced, scientific. In short, this chronic chemical famine may be the cause of the vague sickness, the ill health, the half life—of you and you and you.

You ask: How can I be suffering from chemical starvation when I eat three square meals a day? The new famine-fighting physicians answer that, in the matter of food, nature has played a sinister trick upon her human children. She's stingy with the amount of life-giving B-vitamin chemicals she's put into those foods. Then, to nature's meanness we've added our own stupidity—refining vitamins out of foods in which they were not too plentiful in the first place.

Vitamins keep alight the fire of life. They control, in mysterious ways, the stewings and cookings that go on inside us when we eat. But our body, that wonderful factory for changing bread and meat into tissue, blood, energy, for making no end of complicated chemicals and juices, just doesn't know how to make vitamins. It has to take them from outside, and keep on taking them, for it cannot store them. So no matter what or how much we eat, if vitamins don't come in with the food, we sicken and in time we die.

Out of 1729 victims of various forms of chronic famine, treated at Hillman last year, not one died. No death, mind you, from a chemical starvation that a few years ago killed nearly 50 percent of those ill enough to be hospitalized.

In the hurly-burly of Hillman's Nutrition Clinic you'd never at first glance pick out the director from among the hundreds of patients, nurses, doctors, chemists. Dr. Tom Douglas Spies' coat is off. His collar is open. He wears no tie. Unless you listened to his heart-to-heart talks with his patients, Tom Spies might seem only another husky Texas rancher. But at 38 he's medically world-famous.

Tom Spies' interest in nutrition was first stirred when he was a small boy in Texas and the mother of one of his playmates died of pellagra. After graduating from Harvard Medical School, he became an interne at Lakeside Hospital in Cleveland. There one of his first patients was a pellagrin. It was already well known that pellagra was a deficiency disease, and Spies prescribed the recommended diet. But within 48 hours the patient was dead.

The shock of this led Tom Spies to ten years' investigation of pellagra

17225

and other forms of chronic famine. Reading case histories, he found that 54 percent of those seriously ill died. It occurred to him—this was long before the discovery of the pure vitamin chemicals—that these desperately sick pellagrins weren't getting enough in the curative diet. So he crammed into them huge amounts of food, of wheat germ, yeast, liver extract—and brought the death rate down to six percent. In 1936 Tom Spies was invited to Hillman Hospital to test his massive stuffing treatment on 50 pellagrins, all at the point of death. Only three died—from diseases other than pellagra. This was fine, but the treatment required the constant attention of doctors and nurses, and often six weeks passed before patients could leave the hospital. Dr. Spies was on the watch for the concentrated vitamins themselves.

The first of the pure chemicals came into his hands only a year later, when Wisconsin's Prof. Conrad A. Elvehjem discovered that black tongue—the pellagra of dogs—was cured by nicotinic acid. Two months later Spies announced his rapid cure of desperately sick pellagrins by this same chemical.

After ten years of incessant chemical-starvation hunting, Tom Spies finds each new sufferer as fascinating as the first pellagrin he saved at Lakeside Hospital. He listens to each sick one's story of his jangled chemistry, then links up the tragic chain of events to what he can see— on the backs of their hands, on their tongues, at the corners of their mouths, in their eyes, and by tests of their blood and body fluids.

When the evidence leads him to suspect this, that, or several chemical hungers, he doses his patient boldly with huge amounts of these new magic crystals—the effect of which nobody knew until a few years ago. One of the most miraculously healing of them all, nicotinic acid, though itself harmless, is derived from nicotine, one of the two most deadly of all human poisons. But the patients know Tom Spies would risk nothing on them that he hadn't first tried on himself.

The patients themselves are the most important co-workers in this giant new battle. Hundreds of them, many hardly literate, know they are part of the experiment, and are keenly interested. They are voluntary human guinea pigs for Tom Spies—just because they feel him to be their brother, to be the "old shoe" sort of scientist that's rare in medicine.

In some cases Spies cures his patients, then—and this is fantastic— *un*-cures them, so as to be sure the cure was valid. I talked to Daisy Jones, dragged from the grave by the power of nicotinic acid. Resurrected, she got a job as a social worker. Nothing was said to her at the hospital about the change in diet that would guard her from relapse.

She kept taking tablets of nicotine acid as Tom Spies directed. Then—without her knowing it—tablets of aspirin were substituted. "The doctors saved my life, but I'm not so well; I'm slipping, and I've given up my job," Miss Jones told me. I upbraided Tom Spies for inhumanity. "Don't worry, we'll switch her back to the real stuff and she'll find another job," he said, smiling. She did. She knew what he had done to her, as they all know when at last they are cured.

Two years ago a very sick man came to Hillman Hospital. He couldn't eat, couldn't sleep. He was losing weight and had no strength. His digestion was chronically upset. His eyes itched and burned. There were crawling sensations over his skin and cramps in his leg muscles.

With seeming heartlessness Tom Spies began to work his mercy. He held this deteriorated human experimental animal on his deficient diet. Then our famine fighter began shooting his chemical bullets, one by one, into this ailing body. Each one—with speed and precision new in healing—disposed of this or that particular discomfort, torture, ache. In succession the man was dosed with nicotinic acid, thiamin, riboflavin, pyridoxin, pure Vitamin A, ascorbic acid, and finally adenylic acid. One by one these chemicals made a less and less weak and pain-racked, then a stronger and a better, and at last a new man—of this victim who had suffered seven separate and distinct chemical starvations since childhood.

It seems only yesterday that lack of vitamins—before the chemists had learned to make them—meant only the beriberi of far-off Orientals, only the pellagra or scurvy of a relative handful of our own have-nots. Now, almost overnight, synthetic vitamins bring promise of a new mankind, promise of relief for human failures to which no one had thought of giving a medical name—stupidity, or laziness.

At Hillman Hospital I saw children who might best be described as little sad old men and women when first brought into the Nutrition Clinic. They were always tired, listless, dunces at school. Then I saw them after they had been transformed into mischievous, energetic youngsters, average students—some even into A students heading their classes. Can it be that the so-called "I.Q." is not completely hereditary, but partly chemical? A research into this portentous question is now about to begin in Birmingham.

This much is already known: chemical famine is not confined to the poor. The son of Dr. William MacQueen, Superintendent of Hillman Hospital, was restless, fidgety, unable to concentrate. Doses of thiamin, nicotinic acid, and riboflavin turned him into a different lad.

I saw men who hadn't worked for years, scorned as no-gooders, sent back by these same chemicals to hard work, and liking it. Tom Spies told me of one father of five children, on relief. He couldn't hold a job. He couldn't even walk to look for a job. Now he's a shipbuilder for Uncle Sam, doing heavy lifting, working overtime—thanks to nicotinic acid plus thiamin.

Such people, much more than those insane or dying from pellagra, are a major economic burden on society. If our political leaders would give our famine fighters the means for a scientific Gallup Poll test with these new chemicals, there'd be new light thrown on what's called laziness. And millions now chemically starved would get the energy to find jobs, and from those jobs the food to keep them going.

This stirred me most of all in the Nutrition Clinic at Birmingham: the families of what used to be called "poor white trash." Dr. MacQueen told me he is now convinced that no class of citizens deserves the indignity of that name. Their supposed no-goodness is chemical.

Everybody knows that the various preparations of pure vitamins obtainable in drugstores are beyond the pocketbooks of families with modest incomes as well as of the have-nots. But these magic chemicals are getting cheaper. The chemical industry is swinging into large-scale production and learning to synthesize them from such inexpensive substances as coal tar. Today nearly every ill of mankind, from insanity to cancer, is being subjected to scrutiny by our famine fighters to determine whether chemical starvation is responsible.

The scientists at Hillman Hospital are probably "farthest north" in this exploration. But our men against death, vitamin hunters, chemists—at the Universities of Wisconsin, Illinois, California, Texas, Duke, New York, and in the U. S. Public Health Service—are making similar hopeful forays into what's been a deadly unknown.

Already the new pure Vitamin K is saving babies threatened by internal bleeding. Ascorbic acid relieves some sufferers from a disfiguring skin disease, others from torture from certain kinds of arthritis. Massive doses of the pure E vitamin—tocopherol—check hitherto inexorable nerve degenerations and progressive weakness of muscles. Thiamin dramatically cures delirium tremens.

In laboratories, mice on high vitamin diets can throw off infections fatal to their brothers famished for specific chemicals. Does this prophesy a mankind strong against microbes? Perhaps even armed against infantile paralysis, which now so mysteriously cripples one child while it sickens others for only a few days? These researches are already in progress. Why does one person get old at 40 while another is vigorous at 70? There is already a hint that what keeps senility at bay is the ability of our body to use certain definite chemicals.

So ill after ill, not formerly thought to be caused by hidden chemical starvation, turns out to be that, and that alone. This knowledge marks a revolution in medical science. It may astound us as well as our doctors. But it will hardly surprise our vitamin-hunting chemists. In their laboratories they have already transformed one animal species—the white rat. In length of life, weight, strength, bounding health, they've made a super-rat out of a miserable, ordinary rodent. Will their magic chemicals—when they've found them all and tagged them—give us supermen and women? This is the vista before us today.

At this moment our vitamin hunters are getting set to fight the chronic famine willed by the world's would-be destroyers. Against hidden hunger, here and in Europe, they are working day and night to devise a simple, powerful supercharge of the necessary magic chemicals and minerals. These experiments are not yet ready to be announced. But here's what they have good hope for—

A vitamin supercharge that can be added to a cheap diet of sufficient calories. Two ounces of it per day, spread on a piece of bread, will cost not more than 20 cents a pound. *That's less than ten dollars a year for an abundance of the chemicals essential to human nutrition!*

Last year—in Germany before the blitzkrieg—Tom Spies was informed that the German scientists had concocted a vitamin supercharge for food that would keep the men of the dreaded Panzer divisions alert in their tanks for 72 hours.

The German famine fighters today make supermen—for killing other human beings. Our own vitamin-hunting chemists and physicians, if only the politicians who hold the nation's purse strings will let them, are on the verge of a practical science that will make us into new human beings. Just turn these trail blazers loose in their hospitals and laboratories. They'll make nicotinic acid, thiamin, riboflavin, pyridoxin, ascorbic acid and all the other key life-chemicals so cheap that today's chronic famine—which has kept the poor man weak and the weak man poor—will vanish.

And this strikes home to all of us. Even those of us who can buy all the food we need may yet feel under par, living half lives because of our hidden hunger for certain vitamins. From curing this deterioration among millions to the creation of an American of undreamed-of vigor and energy is a shorter step than many of us now believe.

Even our slightest impulse toward prayer has a dynamic, beneficial effect upon our lives

Prayer Is Power

By Alexis Carrel, M.D.

PRAYER is not only worship; it is also an invisible emanation of man's worshiping spirit—the most powerful form of energy that one can generate. The influence of prayer on the human mind and body is as demonstrable as that of secreting glands. Its results can be measured in terms of increased physical buoyancy, greater intellectual vigor, moral stamina, and a deeper understanding of the realities underlying human relationships.

If you make a habit of sincere prayer, your life will be very noticeably and profoundly altered. Prayer stamps with its indelible mark our actions and demeanor. A tranquility of bearing, a facial and bodily repose, are observed in those whose inner lives are thus enriched. Within the depths of consciousness a flame kindles. And man sees himself. He discovers his selfishness, his silly pride, his fears, his greeds, his blunders. He develops a sense of moral obligation, intellectual humility. Thus begins a journey of the soul toward the realm of grace.

Prayer is a force as real as terrestrial gravity. As a physician, I have seen men, after all other therapy had failed, lifted out of disease and melancholy by the serene effort of prayer. It is the only power in the world that seems to overcome the so-called "laws of nature"; the occasions on which prayer has dramatically done this have been termed "miracles." But a constant, quieter miracle takes place hourly in the hearts of men and women who have discovered that prayer supplies them with a steady flow of sustaining power in their daily lives.

Too many people regard prayer as a formalized routine of words, a refuge for weaklings, or a childish petition for material things. We sadly undervalue prayer when we conceive it in these terms, just as we should

Selected from March 1941 issue of The Reader's Digest

underestimate rain by describing it as something that fills the birdbath in our garden. Properly understood, prayer is a mature activity indispensable to the fullest development of personality—the ultimate integration of man's highest faculties. Only in prayer do we achieve that complete and harmonious assembly of body, mind and spirit which gives the frail human reed its unshakable strength.

The words, "Ask and it shall be given to you," have been verified by the experience of humanity. True, prayer may not restore the dead child to life or bring relief from physical pain. But prayer, like radium, is a source of luminous, self-generating energy.

How does prayer fortify us with so much dynamic power? To answer this question (admittedly outside the jurisdiction of science) I must point out that all prayers have one thing in common. The triumphant hosannas of a great oratorio, or the humble supplication of an Iroquois hunter begging for luck in the chase, demonstrate the same truth: that human beings seek to augment their finite energy by addressing themselves to the Infinite source of all energy. When we pray, we link ourselves with the inexhaustible motive power that spins the universe. We ask that a part of this power be apportioned to our needs. Even in asking, our human deficiencies are filled and we arise strengthened and repaired.

But we must never summon God merely for the gratification of our whims. We derive most power from prayer when we use it, not as a petition, but as a supplication that we may become more like Him. Prayer should be regarded as practice of the Presence of God. An old peasant was seated alone in the last pew of the village church. "What are you waiting for?" he was asked; and he answered, "I am looking at Him and He is looking at me." Man prays not only that God should remember him, but also that he should remember God.

How can prayer be defined? Prayer is the effort of man to reach God, to commune with an invisible being, creator of all things, supreme wisdom, truth, beauty, and strength, father and redeemer of each man. This goal of prayer always remains hidden to intelligence. For both language and thought fail when we attempt to describe God.

We do know, however, that whenever we

address God in fervent prayer we change both soul and body for the better. It could not happen that any man or woman could pray for a single moment without some good result. "No man ever prayed," said Emerson, "without learning something."

One can pray everywhere. In the streets, the subway, the office, the shop, the school, as well as in the solitude of one's own room or among the crowd in a church. There is no prescribed posture, time or place.

"Think of God more often than you breathe," said Epictetus the Stoic. In order really to mold personality, prayer must become a habit. It is meaningless to pray in the morning and to live like a barbarian the remainder of the day. True prayer is a way of life; the truest life is literally a way of prayer.

The best prayers are like the improvisations of gifted lovers, always about the same thing yet never twice the same. We cannot all be as creative in prayer as Saint Theresa or Bernard of Clairvaux, both of whom poured their adoration into words of mystical beauty. Fortunately, we do not need their eloquence; our slightest impulse to prayer is recognized by God. Even if we are pitifully dumb, or if our tongues are overlaid with vanity or deceit, our meager syllables of praise are acceptable to Him, and He showers us with strengthening manifestations of His love.

Today, as never before, prayer is a binding necessity in the lives of men and nations. The lack of emphasis on the religious sense has brought the world to the edge of destruction. Our deepest source of power and perfection has been left miserably undeveloped. Prayer, the basic exercise of the spirit, must be actively practiced in our private lives. The neglected soul of man must be made strong enough to assert itself once more. For if the power of prayer is again released and used in the lives of common men and women; if the spirit declares its aims clearly and boldly, there is yet hope that our prayers for a better world will be answered.

DR. ALEXIS CARREL has long been impressed by the fact that many of life's phenomena cannot be scientifically explained. He knows, for example, that miracles of healing are possible; he spent weeks at Lourdes studying them, and will never forget seeing a cancerous sore shrivel to a scar before his eyes. Dr. Carrel concluded 33 years of brilliant biological research at the Rockefeller Institute in 1939. Among his many honors are the Nordhoff-Jung medal for cancer research and the Nobel Prize for success in suturing blood vessels. His *Man, the Unknown* was a best seller in 1935.

MADAME CURIE

A condensation from the book by

EVE CURIE

DAUGHTER OF MADAME CURIE

Translated by Vincent Sheean

"It would have been a crime to add the slightest ornament to this story of my mother, so like a myth," writes Eve Curie. "I have not related a single anecdote of which I am not sure or so much as invented the color of a dress. The facts are as stated; the quoted words were actually pronounced.

"I hope that the reader may feel what in Marie was even more rare than her work or her life: the immovable structure of a character; the quality of a soul in which neither fame nor adversity could change the exceptional purity. A quality which made Einstein say of her: 'Marie Curie is, of all celebrated beings, the only one whom fame has not corrupted.'"

MADAME CURIE

IN THE FALL of 1891 a young Polish *émigrée* named Marie Sklodovska excitedly registered for the science course at the Sorbonne in Paris.

Often in the echoing galleries young men would encounter this shy and stubborn-faced girl who dressed with poverty-stricken austerity, and would ask: "Who is it?" But the answer was vague. "It's a foreigner with an impossible name. She is always in the first row at the physics courses." The boys' eyes would follow her graceful outline down the corridor, and they would conclude: "Fine hair!" The ash-blonde hair and the little Slavic head were, for a long time, the only identification the students at the Sorbonne had for their timid comrade.

But young men were what interested this girl least. She was entirely fascinated by her scientific studies and worked as if in a fever. Every minute she did not consecrate to study was a minute lost.

Too shy to make friends with the French, Marie Sklodovska took refuge among her compatriots in the colony which formed a little island of free Poland in the Latin Quarter of Paris. There her life was one of monastic simplicity. Her income—made up by her own savings from her work as a governess in Poland, and the small sums her father, an obscure but cultured teacher of mathematics, could send her—was but 40 rubles a month. From this stipend—*three francs* a day—she had to pay for her room, meals, clothes, and expenses at the university.

By deliberate intention she suppressed diversions from her schedule, as well as friendly meetings, and made for herself a Spartan existence, strange and inhuman. Marie did not admit that she could be cold or hungry. In order not to buy coal she often neglected to light her little stove, and she wrote figures and equations without noticing that her fingers were numb and her shoulders shaking. For weeks at a time she ate nothing but buttered bread and tea. When she wanted a feast, she bought two eggs, or a piece of chocolate or some fruit.

From MADAME CURIE, a biography, by Eve Curie.
Copyright 1937, by Doubleday Doran and Company, Inc.

On this diet the fresh, solid girl who had left Warsaw a few months before rapidly grew anemic. Often, as she was getting up from her table, her head would go round. She had just time to get to her bed when she would lose consciousness. Coming to, she would ask why she had fainted; she would think herself ill and disdain her illness as she did everything else that interfered with her work. It never occurred to her at such times that her only disease was starvation.

Pierre Curie

MARIE had ruled love and marriage out of her life's program. Dominated by the passion for science, at 26 she still clung fiercely to her independence.

Then came Pierre Curie. A French scientist of genius, he was devoting body and soul to scientific research, and was unmarried at 35. He was tall, possessed long sensitive hands, a rough beard, and an expression of rare intelligence and distinction.

Their first meeting occurred in 1894 in the laboratory, and immediate sympathy brought them together. Pierre Curie found this taciturn Mlle. Sklodovska truly an astonishing person. How strange to talk to a young and charming woman, using technical terms, complicated formulae. . . . How sweet it was!

Pierre looked at Marie's ash-blonde hair, at her high, curved forehead and her hands already stained by the acids of the laboratory. He was disconcerted by her grace, which the absence of all coquetry made more surprising.

Pierre Curie, with gentle tenacity, endeavored to get on friendly terms with the girl. He asked if he could visit her. Friendly but reserved, she received him in her little room, and Pierre, his heart constricted by so much poverty, nevertheless appreciated the subtle agreement between character and setting. In an almost empty attic, with her threadbare dress and her ardent, stubborn features, Marie had never seemed more beautiful. What fascinated him was not only her total devotion to her work, but also her courage and nobility. This graceful girl had the character and gifts of a great man.

In a few months Pierre Curie asked Marie to be his wife. But to marry a Frenchman, leave her family forever, and to abandon her beloved oppressed Poland, seemed to Mlle. Sklodovska like dreadful acts of betrayal. Ten months had to pass before the obdurate Pole accepted the idea of marriage.

THE FIRST days of their life together Pierre and Marie roamed the Ile-de-France on bicycles purchased with money given them as a wedding present. They lunched on bread and cheese and fruit, stopped at hazard in unknown inns, and at the cost of some thousands of pedal strokes and a few francs for village lodgings, attained the luxury of solitude for long enchanted days and nights.

The little flat at 24 rue de la Glacière, where the young couple settled, was singularly lacking in comfort, and they refused the furniture offered them by Pierre's father. Marie hadn't the time to clean it. The bare walls were furnished only with books, two chairs, and a white wooden table. On the table were treatises on physics, a petroleum lamp, a bunch of flowers: and that was all. Before these two chairs, neither of which was for him, the most daring visitor could only flee.

Little by little Marie improved in housekeeping wisdom. She invented dishes which needed little preparation, or could be left to "cook themselves." Before going out, Marie would regulate the flame with a physicist's precision: then, casting one last worried glance at the stewpans she was entrusting to the fire, she flew down the stairs and caught up with her husband. In a quarter of an hour, bent over other containers, she would regulate the flame on a laboratory burner with the same careful gesture.

The second year of their marriage differed from the first only in Marie's health, which was upset by her pregnancy. Mme. Curie had wanted a child, but she was vexed at being so ill that she was unable to stand before the apparatus and study the magnetization of steel.

It might be supposed that Pierre would be so softened by Marie's condition as to pass a quiet summer with her; not so. With the thoughtlessness of the insane, the pair went off to Brest on their bicycles during her eighth month of pregnancy, covering stages as long as they usually did. Marie declared that she felt no fatigue, and Pierre had a vague feeling that she was a supernatural being, who escaped from human laws.

Soon, however, the young wife was forced, in great humiliation, to cut short the trip and go back to Paris, where she gave birth to a daughter: Irène, a beautiful baby and a future Nobel prize winner.

The idea of choosing between family and the scientific career did not even cross Marie's mind. She kept house, washed her baby daughter and put pans on the fire, but she also kept on working in a wretched laboratory—working toward the most important discovery of modern science.

The Discovery of Radium

AT THE END of 1897 the balance sheet of Marie's activity showed two university degrees, a fellowship and a monograph on the magnetization of tempered steel. The next goal was the doctor's degree. Casting about for a research project for this, Marie was attracted by a recent publication of the French scientist Henri Becquerel.

Becquerel had discovered that uranium salts *spontaneously* emitted, without exposure to light, rays of unknown nature. A compound of uranium, placed on a photographic plate surrounded by black paper, made an impression on the plate through the paper. It was the first observation of the phenomenon, which Marie later named *radioactivity,* but the nature and origin of the radiation remained an enigma.

Becquerel's discovery fascinated the Curies. They asked themselves whence came the energy which uranium compounds constantly disengaged as radiation. Here was an engrossing subject of research—a leap into an unknown realm.

There remained the question of where to make her experiments—and here the difficulties began. At last, thanks to the director of the School of Physics where Pierre taught, Marie was given the use of a little ground-floor storeroom, sweating with damp, where unused machines were put away.

Scientific research in this hole was not easy. And the climate there, fatal to sensitive precision instruments, was not much better for Marie's health. But this had no importance. When she was cold, she took her revenge by savagely noting the degrees of temperature in her notebook.

The more Marie penetrated into intimacy with uranium rays, the more they seemed without precedent, essentially unknown. Presently, by undertaking the laborious examination of all known chemical bodies, she discovered that compounds of another element, thorium, also emitted spontaneous rays like those of uranium. Moreover, in each case the radioactivity was a great deal stronger than seemed warranted by the uranium or thorium contained in the products examined!

Where did this abnormal radiation come from? Only one explanation was possible: the minerals must contain, in small quantity, a *much more powerfully radioactive substance* than uranium and thorium. But what substance? In her experiments, Marie had examined *all known chemical elements*. The scientist replied to the question with the magnificent audaciousness of a great mind: The minerals certainly contained a radioactive substance, which must be a hitherto unknown chemical element.

A new element! It was a fascinating hypothesis. But the incognito of the wonderful substance had to be broken. She must be able to announce with certainty: "It is there."

Pierre Curie, who had followed the rapid progress of his wife's experiments with passionate interest, now abandoned his own experiments in order to aid hers. Two brains, four hands, now sought the unknown element in the damp little workroom, and a collaboration began which was to last eight years, until it was destroyed by a fatal accident.

Marie and Pierre began their prospecting patiently, separating and measuring the radioactivity of all the elements in pitchblende, an ore of uranium. But as the field of investigation narrowed, their findings indicated the existence of two new elements instead of one. By July, 1898, they were able to announce the discovery of one of these substances. Marie named it *polonium,* after her beloved Poland.

In December, 1898, the Curies announced the existence of a second new chemical element in pitchblende which they called *radium*—an element whose radioactivity they believed to be enormous.

Genius—in a Shed

THE SPECIAL properties of radium upset fundamental theories in which scientists had believed for centuries, and physicists received the discovery with reserve. The attitude of the chemists was even more downright. By definition, a chemist believes in the existence of a new substance only when he has seen and examined it, confronted it with acids, and determined its atomic weight.

Now, nobody had ever seen radium. Nobody knew its atomic weight. To prove the existence of polonium and radium, the Curies were now to labor for four years. They knew how they hoped to isolate the new metals, but it meant handling large quantities of crude material.

Pitchblende, in which polonium and radium were hidden, was treated at the St. Joachimsthal mines in Bohemia to extract uranium salts used in making glass. It was a costly ore, but according to the Curies' calculations, the extraction of uranium should leave polonium and radium intact. Then why not work the residue?

From the Austrian government they obtained a ton of the residue, and began work on it in an abandoned shed close by the little room where Marie had done her first experiments. The Faculty of Medicine had formerly used the place as a dissecting room, but now it was not even considered fit to house cadavers. It had no floor and was furnished with some worn kitchen tables, a blackboard and an old cast-iron stove.

In the summer the shed was as stifling as a hothouse. In winter the stove, even when stoked white, left a zone of ice. However, since their technical installation possessed no chimneys to carry off noxious gases, the greater part of their treatment was made in the courtyard outside.

"And yet," Marie wrote later, "it was in this miserable old shed that the best and happiest years of our life were spent, entirely consecrated to work. I sometimes passed the whole day stirring a mass in ebullition, with an iron rod nearly as big as myself. In the evening I was entirely broken with fatigue."

In such conditions M. and Mme. Curie worked from 1898 to 1902. In that courtyard, dressed in her old dust-covered and acid-stained smock, her hair blown by the wind, surrounded by bitter smoke which stung her eyes and throat, Marie was a virtual factory all by herself.

"I came to treat as many as 20 kilograms of matter at a time," she writes, "which had the effect of filling the shed with great jars of precipitates and liquids. It was killing work to carry the receivers, to pour off the liquids and to stir, for hours at a stretch, the boiling matter in a smelting basin."

The days of work became months and years: Pierre and Marie were not discouraged. Sometimes, when they left their apparatus for a moment, their talk about their beloved radium passed from the transcendent to the childish.

"I wonder what *It* will look like," Marie said one day with the feverish curiosity of a child who has been promised a toy. "Pierre, what form do you imagine *It* will take?"

"I don't know," the physicist answered gently. "I should like it to have a very beautiful color. . . ."

As Marie, with terrible patience, continued to treat, kilogram by kilogram, the tons of pitchblende residue sent from St. Joachimsthal, the old tables in the shed held products more and more concentrated— more and more rich in radium. She was approaching the end: she was now at the stage of purification of strongly radioactive solutions. But the poverty of her haphazard equipment hindered her work more than ever. In this shed, open to every wind, iron and coal dust was afloat which, to Marie's despair, mixed itself into the products purified with so much care. Her heart sometimes constricted before these little daily accidents, which took so much of her time and strength.

Pierre was so tired of the interminable struggle that he would have abandoned it for the time being. The obstacles seemed insurmountable. Could they not resume this work later on, under better conditions?

He counted without his wife's character. Marie wanted to isolate radium and she would isolate it. She scorned fatigue and difficulties and even the gaps in her own knowledge which complicated her task. After all, she was only a very young scientist: and sometimes she stumbled across phenomena or methods of calculation of which she knew very little, and for which she had to make hasty studies.

In 1902, 45 months after the day on which the Curies announced the probable existence of radium, Marie, by superhuman obstinacy, finally achieved victory: she succeeded in preparing a decigram of pure radium and determined its atomic weight.

The chemists could only bow before the facts. Radium officially existed.

A Hard Life

UNFORTUNATELY, the Curies had other struggles than that with Nature in their poor laboratory. Pierre's salary at the School of Physics was 500 francs a month and after Irène's birth the cost of a nurse made heavy inroads on the budget. New resources had to be found.

In 1898, a chair of physical chemistry fell vacant at the Sorbonne and Pierre decided to ask for it. It paid 10,000 francs and would mean fewer hours of lessons; but his candidature was rejected. Pierre was to obtain the post of professor only in 1904, after the whole world had acclaimed his worth. For the present he had to accept an inferior position at the Sorbonne, where the authorities were only too willing to entrust him with time-filling lessons of secondary importance. Meanwhile Marie secured a professorship at a girls' school near Versailles.

The budget was now balanced, but the Curies were burdened with an enormous increase of work at the exact moment when their experiments in radioactivity called for all their energy. Pierre's friends sought by all means to bring him a little nearer to that inaccessible place of Professor. Membership in the Academy of Sciences would greatly enhance his prestige, and in 1902 they insisted on making Pierre present himself as a candidate. He hesitated, and then obeyed without pleasure. He found it hard to make the customary visits to the academicians. And to set forth his honors, state the good opinion he had of himself, boast of his work, seemed beyond his power. Consequently he eulogized his opponent, saying that M. Amagat was much better qualified than he to enter the Institute. . . . The academicians chose M. Amagat.

Shortly thereafter, Pierre refused to be named for the Legion of Honor. It seemed too comic that a scientist, refused the means of work-

114

ing, should by way of "encouragement" be offered a cross on a red ribbon.

The Curies continued to teach, with a good will and without bitterness, giving to the job their best efforts. And torn between their own work and their jobs, they forgot to eat and sleep. Unconscious of their folly, the pair abused their ebbing strength. On several occasions Pierre was obliged to take to his bed by attacks of intolerable pain in the legs. Marie was upheld by her tense nerves from a breakdown, but friends were startled by the pallor and emaciation of her face.

Thus radioactivity grew and developed, meanwhile exhausting little by little the pair of physicists who had given it life.

A Decision "of No Importance"

PRODIGIOUS radium! Purified as a chloride, it appeared to be a dull white powder, much like common kitchen salt. But its properties were stupefying. Its radiation passed all expectation in intensity; it proved to be two million times stronger than that of uranium. The rays traversed the hardest and most opaque matter. Only a thick screen of lead proved able to stop their insidious penetration.

The last and most moving miracle was that radium could become the ally of human beings in the war against cancer. Radium was *useful—* magnificently useful, and its extraction no longer had merely experimental interest. A radium industry was about to be born.

Since the therapeutic effects of radium had become known, plans for exploitation of radioactive ores had been made, particularly in Belgium and in America. But engineers could produce the "fabulous metal" only if they knew the secret of the delicate operations involved.

Pierre explained these things to his wife one Sunday morning. He had just finished reading a letter from some technicians in the United States who wanted to exploit radium in America, and asked for information.

"We have two choices," Pierre told her. "We can describe our results without reserve, including the processes of purification . . ."

Marie made a mechanical gesture of approval and murmured:

"Yes, naturally."

"Or else," Pierre went on, "we can consider ourselves to be the proprietors, the 'inventors' of radium, patent the technique of treating pitchblende, and assure ourselves of rights over the manufacture of radium throughout the world."

Marie reflected a few seconds. Then she said:

"It is impossible. It would be contrary to the scientific spirit."

Pierre's serious face lightened. To settle his conscience, he dwelt upon it, mentioning the only thing which it was cruel for him to give up:

"We could have a fine laboratory too."

Marie's gaze grew fixed. She steadily considered this idea of gain. Almost at once she rejected it.

"Physicists always publish their researches completely. If our discovery has a commercial future, that is an accident by which we must not profit. And radium is going to be of use in treating disease. . . . It is impossible to take advantage of that."

She made no attempt to convince her husband; she guessed that he had spoken of the patent only out of scruple. Her words expressed the feelings of both, their infallible conception of the scientist's rôle.

Pierre added, as if settling a question of no importance:

"I shall write tonight, then, to the American engineers, and give them the information they ask for."

A quarter of an hour after this little Sunday-morning talk, Pierre and Marie headed for the woods on their beloved bicycles. They had chosen forever between poverty and fortune. In the evening they came back exhausted, their arms filled with leaves and field flowers.

The Enemy

Now came the prelude to the symphony soon to approach its crescendo.

In June, 1903, the Royal Institution officially invited Pierre to London to lecture on radium. Following this came a deluge of invitations, for all London wanted to see the parents of radium.

The Curies uneasily endured this for a few days, then went back to their shed. But the Anglo-Saxons are faithful to those they admire. In November, 1903, the Royal Society of London bestowed on Pierre and Marie one of its highest awards: the Davy Medal.

Next, recognition came from Sweden. On December 10, 1903, the Academy of Science of Stockholm announced that the Nobel Prize in Physics for the current year was awarded half to Henri Becquerel, half to M. and Mme. Curie for their discoveries in radioactivity.

This Nobel Prize meant 70,000 gold francs, and it was not "contrary to the scientific spirit" to accept it. A unique chance to release Pierre from his hours of teaching, to save his health! When the blessed check was paid, there were presents and loans to Pierre's brother, to Marie's sisters, subscriptions to scientific societies, gifts to Polish students, to a childhood friend of Marie's.

Marie also installed a "modern" bathroom in their little house and repapered a shabby room. But it never entered her head to mark the occasion by buying a new hat. And she kept on with her teaching, although she insisted on Pierre's leaving the School of Physics.

When fame opened her arms to them, telegrams piled up on the huge worktable, there were newspaper articles by thousands, hundreds of requests for autographs and photographs, letters from inventors, poems on radium. An American even wanted to name a race horse after Marie.

But a permanent misunderstanding separated the Curies from the public which now turned toward them. They had reached a moment which was perhaps the most pathetic of their lives: for their mission was not finished; they wanted only to work.

But fame took little account of the future toward which Pierre and Marie were straining. Fame leaps upon the great, hangs its full weight upon them, attempts to arrest their development.

The publicity of the Nobel Prize caused millions to consign radioactivity, although still in an embryonic stage, to the class of achieved victories; and they busied themselves in breaking in upon the intimacy of the already legendary couple. This homage dispossessed the Curies of the only treasures they wished to keep: meditation and silence.

As Marie wrote in the spring of 1904:

> . . . Always a hubbub. People are keeping us from work as much as they can. Now I have decided to be brave and I receive no visitors—but they disturb me just the same. Our life has been altogether spoiled by honors and fame. . . . Our peaceful and laborious existence is completely disorganized.

Marie suffered particularly from the part the world wished her to play; her nature was so exacting that among all the attitudes suggested by fame she could choose none: neither familiarity nor mechanical friendliness, deliberate austerity nor showy modesty. She did not know how to be famous. An irresistible timidity congealed her as soon as curious glances were fastened upon her.

One anecdote out of a thousand sums up beautifully the response of the Curies to public acclaim. The couple were dining at the Elysée Palace with President and Mme. Loubet. In the course of the evening Mme. Loubet asked Marie:

"Would you like me to present you to the King of Greece?"

Marie, innocently and politely, replied, all too sincerely:

"I don't see the utility of it." Then, perceiving the lady's stupefaction, she blushed and said precipitately:

"But—but—naturally, I shall do whatever you please. Just as you please."

In compensation for the disaster fame wrought in their lives, it should have brought the Curies certain advantages: the professorship, the laboratory, the collaborators and the credits so long desired. But when would these benefactions come?

Side by Side

WHEN the end of her second pregnancy arrived in 1904, Marie was near exhaustion. The lying-in was painful, interminable. Finally, on December 6, 1904, a plump baby was born, crowned with shaggy black hair. Another daughter: Eve.*

Marie soon resumed the routine of school and laboratory. The couple were never seen in society. But they could not always get out of official banquets in honor of foreign scientists. On such occasions Pierre would don his shiny tails and Marie would put on her one evening dress.

This dress, which she kept for years, to be transformed from time to time by a dressmaker, was made of black grenadine. A smart woman would have looked upon it with pity. But the discretion and reserve which were the very mark of Marie's character created a sort of style in her dress. When she wound her ash-blonde hair into a crest and timidly hung a light necklace of gold filigree about her neck, she was exquisite. Her slender body and inspired face suddenly unveiled their charm.

"It's a pity," Pierre murmured once. "Evening dress becomes you!" With a sigh, he added: "But there it is, we haven't got time."

On July 3, 1905, Pierre Curie entered the Academy—but only just! Twenty-two scientists voted for his opponent. Meanwhile the Sorbonne had created a chair in physics for him—the post so long desired—but still there was no adequate laboratory.

Eight more years of patience were required before Marie was to install radioactivity in a dwelling worthy of it—a dwelling which Pierre was never to see. The harrowing idea that her companion had waited in vain for his beautiful laboratory—the single ambition of his life—until the very end, was to live with her always.

> "Madame Curie and I are working," wrote Pierre on April 14, 1906, "to dose radium with precision by the amount of emanation it gives off. That might seem to be nothing, and yet here we have been at it for several months and are only now beginning to obtain regular results."

* The author.

Madame Curie and I are working . . .

These words, written by Pierre five days before his death, express the essence and the beauty of a union which was never weakened. Each progress of the work, each of their disappointments and victories, linked this husband and wife more closely together.

Between these two equals who admired each other passionately but could never envy, there was a worker's comradeship, light and exquisite, which was perhaps the most delicate expression of their profound love.

Alone

TOWARDS half-past two on Thursday, April 19, 1906—a sultry, rainy day—Pierre took leave of the professors in the Faculty of Science, with whom he had been lunching, and went out into the downpour. As he attempted to cross the rue Dauphine, Pierre absent-mindedly stepped from behind a cab into the path of a heavy dray. Surprised, he attempted to hang on to the chest of the horse, which suddenly reared. The scientist's heels slipped on the wet pavement. The driver pulled on the reins, but in vain: the enormous wagon, dragged on by its weight of six tons, continued for several yards. The left back wheel encountered a feeble obstacle which it crushed in passing. Policemen picked up the warm body, from which life had been taken away in a flash.

Six o'clock: Marie, gay and vivid, appeared in the doorway of her home. She found callers, and vaguely perceived, in their too-deferential attitude, the signs of compassion. As they gave an account of the facts, Marie remained motionless. Her lips moved at last:

"Pierre is dead? Dead? Absolutely dead?"

From the moment when those three words, "Pierre is dead," reached her consciousness, she became a pitiful and incurably lonely woman.

In a few laconic words she asked that Pierre's body be brought home. She begged a friend to take Irène; she sent a brief telegram to her father in Warsaw. Then she went out into the wet garden and sat down, her head in her hands, her gaze empty. Deaf, inert, mute, she waited for her companion.

Slowly, painfully, the stretcher was edged through the narrow door. The dead man was stretched out in a room on the ground floor, and Marie remained alone with her husband. She kissed his face, his supple body, still almost warm. She was taken by force into another room so as not to be present at the dressing of the body. She obeyed, as if unconscious, and then seized by the idea that she had allowed herself to be robbed of these minutes, she came back and clung to the body.

After the funeral, the government officially proposed to award the widow and children of Pierre Curie a national pension. Marie refused flatly: "I don't want a pension," she said. "I am young enough to earn my living and that of my children."

On May 13, 1906, the council of the Faculty of Science unanimously decided to confide Pierre's chair at the Sorbonne to Marie. For the first time a position in French higher education had been given to a woman.

Marie listened distractedly, almost with indifference, to her father-in-law giving the details of the heavy mission she owed it to herself to accept. She answered in a few syllables: "I will try."

On the day of her first lecture at the Sorbonne, the crowd filled the little graded amphitheater and overflowed into the corridors and the square outside. Necks were craned so as not to miss Mme. Curie's entrance. What would be the new professor's first words? Would she thank the Minister, the university? Would she speak of Pierre? Yes, undoubtedly: the custom was to begin with a eulogy of one's predecessor....

Half-past one. . . . The door at the back opened, and Marie Curie walked to the chair in a storm of applause. She inclined her head. It was a dry little movement intended as a salute. Standing, Marie waited for the ovation to cease. It ceased suddenly.

Marie stared straight ahead of her and said: "When one considers the progress that has been made in physics in the past ten years, one is surprised at the advance that has taken place in our ideas concerning electricity and matter. . . ."

Mme. Curie had resumed the course at the sentence where Pierre Curie had left it. Tears rose to the eyes and fell upon the faces there.

Having reached the end of her arid exposition without flinching, Marie retired by the little door as rapidly as she had come in.

Successes and Ordeals

Now the personal fame of Mme. Curie mounted and spread like a rocket. Diplomas and honors from foreign academies arrived by the dozen. And although the Academy of Sciences failed to honor her with membership—Marie missed being elected by one vote—Sweden awarded her the Nobel Prize in Chemistry for the year 1911. No other man or woman has ever received such a recompense twice.

The Sorbonne and the Pasteur Institute jointly founded the Institute of Radium, comprised of two parts: a laboratory of radioactivity, directed by Marie Curie; and a laboratory for biological research and the study of cancer treatment, directed by an eminent physician. Against the advice of the family, Marie made the laboratory a gift of the gram of radium, worth more than a million gold francs, which she and Pierre had prepared with their own hands. To the end of her life this laboratory remained the center of her existence.

When the war came, Marie took up wholeheartedly the service of her second fatherland. Discovering that the hospitals lacked adequate X-ray equipment with which to locate shell fragments and bullets in the wounded, she immediately recognized her field: many radiological stations must be created at once. She went to the manufacturers and university laboratories, collected all the usuable X-ray apparatus and distributed it to the hospitals near Paris. Volunteer operators were recruited among the professors, engineers and scientists.

For ambulance work near the front, Marie created, with funds from the Union of Women of France, the first "radiological car": an automobile with a Roentgen apparatus and a dynamo, driven by the car motor. This complete mobile post, the only one available during the Battle of the Marne, moved from hospital to hospital from August, 1914, onward.

Later more of these cars, nicknamed "little Curies," were equipped by Marie, one by one. She nagged at the sluggish officials, demanded passes and requisitions, until 20 cars were in service. One of them she herself often manned at the front. Aside from this, Marie installed 200 radiological rooms. The total number of wounded men examined by these 220 posts, fixed or mobile, went above a million.

Indifferent to the lack of comfort, she asked for no particular consideration in this work. She spoke neither of fatigue, nor of the cruel effect of X-rays upon herself, nor of the risk of death under fire. For her exceptional war service Marie received no citation; but she was conscious of having served France as best she could.

America

IN 1920 the women of America raised $100,000 to buy a gram of radium for Marie Curie. In exchange they asked her to visit them.

Marie hesitated. But, touched by the magnificent generosity, she conquered her fears and accepted for the first time, at 54, the obligations of a great official journey.

At the landing pier in New York an enormous mob waited for her five hours. From the moment of her arrival it was apparent how much the timid Mme. Curie meant to America. Even before knowing her, the Americans had surrounded her with an almost religious devotion; now that she was here among them, their homage was boundless.

I cannot pretend to define the soul of a people; but the irrepressible rush of enthusiasm with which the United States welcomed Marie Curie was not without its profound meaning. The Latin peoples grant the Americans practical genius, but, by singular vanity, reserve to themselves a monopoly upon idealism. Nevertheless it was a wave of idealism that broke at the feet of Marie Curie. A Mme. Curie sure of herself, haughty, enriched by her discoveries, might perhaps have provoked curiosity; but she would not have aroused this collective tenderness. Above and beyond the frightened scientist, the Americans were acclaiming an attitude toward life which moved them deeply: the scorn for gain, devotion to an intellectual passion, and the desire to serve.

All the universities of America had invited Mme. Curie to visit them. Medals, honorary titles and degrees were awaiting her by the dozen. But she was stunned by the noise and the acclamations. The staring of innumerable people frightened her, as did the violent jostling to get a look at her. She was vaguely afraid of being crushed in one of these terrible eddies. Eventually she became too weak to continue her journey, and on the advice of her doctors she returned to France.

Marie was very tired and very content. The most stubborn modesty could not conceal from her the fact that her personal success in the United States had been enormous.

I believe the journey to America taught my mother that her determined isolation was paradoxical. As a research worker she might cut herself off from the century and concentrate entirely on her own work. But Mme. Curie at 55 was something other than a research worker: The prestige of her name was such that by her mere presence, she could assure the success of some project dear to her. From now on she was to reserve a place in her life for these missions.

Her journeys now were much alike. Scientific congresses, lectures, university ceremonies and visits to laboratories called Mme. Curie to a large number of capitals. She was fêted and acclaimed in them all. She tried to make herself useful. Too often she was obliged to struggle against her uncertain health.

By popular collection Warsaw built a radium institute—the Marie Sklodovska-Curie Institute. The women of America accomplished a new miracle by collecting the money for the purchase of a gram of radium for it—the second gram given by America to Mme. Curie. The events of 1921 repeated themselves: in October, 1929, she again sailed for New York, to thank America in the name of Poland. She was the guest of President Hoover and stayed at the White House several days.

But nothing in her had changed; neither the physical fear of crowds nor her incurable inaptitude for vanity. In spite of a loyal effort, Marie did not succeed in making her pact with fame. It was always the laboratory—and its young scientists—that held first place in Marie Curie's heart. "I don't know whether I could live without the laboratory," she once wrote.

To understand this confession we must see Marie Curie at her apparatus. No exceptional experiment was necessary to give her features a sublime expression of absorption and ecstasy. A difficult piece of glassblower's work that Marie brought off like an artist, a measurement well made, could give her immense joy. If an experiment failed, she seemed thunderstruck by disaster. Seated on a chair, her arms crossed, her back humped, her gaze empty, she suggested some old peasant woman, mute and desolate in a great grief.

The End of a Mission

To THE END of her life Marie continued to work with singular haste—and with the singular imprudence which was usual with her. She had always scorned the precautions which she so severely imposed on her pupils: to manipulate tubes of radioactive bodies with pincers, never to touch unguarded tubes, to use leaden "bucklers" to ward off the harmful radiations. She barely consented to submit to the blood tests which were the rule at the Institute of Radium. Her blood content was abnormal. What of it? . . . For 35 years Mme. Curie had handled radium and breathed the emanation of radium. During the four years of the war she had been exposed to the even more dangerous radiation of the Roentgen apparatus. Slight deterioration in the blood, annoying and painful burns on the hands, were not, after all, such very severe punishments for the number of risks she had run!

Marie paid little attention to the light fever which began to trouble her. But in May, 1934, she took to her bed after an attack of the grippe and did not leave it again. When at last the robust heart beat no more, science pronounced its verdict. The abnormal symptoms, the strange, unprecedented blood tests, accused the true criminal: radium.

On Friday, July 6, 1934, at noon, without speeches or processions, without a politician or an official present, Mme. Curie modestly took her place in the realm of the dead. She was buried beside Pierre in the cemetery at Sceaux in the presence of her relatives, her friends, and the co-workers who loved her.